D0605386

APR 2 5 2012

NO LONGER PROPERTY OF
SEATTLE PUBLIC LIBRARY

Antony Worrall Thompson

The Essential
Low Fat Cookbook

Good healthy eating for every day

with an introduction by
Juliette Kellow BSc RD

Photography by Georgia Glynn Smith

Kyle Books

Published in 2012 by Kyle Books
an imprint of Kyle Cathie Limited
www.kylebooks.com

Distributed by National Book Network
4501 Forbes Blvd., Suite 200
Lanham, MD 20706
Phone: (800) 462-6420
Fax: (301) 429-5746
custserv@nbnbooks.com

First published in Great Britain in 2011 by Kyle Books

10 9 8 7 6 5 4 3 2 1

ISBN 978-1-906868-52-9

All rights reserved. No reproduction, copy or transmission of this publication may
be made without written permission. No paragraph of this publication may be
reproduced, copied or transmitted save with written permission or in accordance
with the provision of the Copyright Act 1956 (as amended). Any person who does any
unauthorised act in relation to this publication may be liable to criminal prosecution
and civil claims for damages.

Antony Worrall Thompson is hereby identified as the author of this work in accordance
with Section 77 of the Copyright, Designs and Patents Act 1988.

Text © 2011 Antony Worrall Thompson

Book design © 2011 Kyle Cathie Limited

Project editor: Judith Hannam
Photographer: Georgia Glynn Smith
Food stylist: Aya Nishimura
Props stylist: Nadine Tubbs
Designer: Jacqui Caulton
Editorial assistants: Elanor Clarke and Laura Foster
Production: Gemma John
Copy editor: Emily Hatchwell
Proof reader: Clare Hubbard
Indexer: Helen Snaith

Library of Congress Control Number: 2011940443

Printed and bound by 1010 Printing International Ltd

Dedication

To Paul Mullen

who needs to eat

more food like this...

he know's it,

and he's a great cook.

Contents

Foreword by HEART UK

The Cholesterol Charity

It is refreshing to see *The Essential Low Fat Cookbook* in print, proving that indulgent food can be appetizing and enjoyable, even if it is not loaded with fat, salt, and sugar. Juliette Kellow provides a wonderful introduction to this book, detailing the reasons why we should all limit our fat intake.

Eating healthily is not only about watching your total fat intake; it's also about the quality and balance of fats in your diet. As a first step, cutting back on saturated fat is the best way to limit total fat intake. For positive heart health, and whenever you use fats in cooking, health professionals recommend you use seed, nut, and vegetable oils as these provide vital mono- and polyunsaturated fatty acids. As Juliette points out on page 26, you should still limit the amount of these oils that you use in your cooking, because they are concentrated sources of both fat and calories. Not only do Antony Worrall Thompson's magnificent recipes make it easy for the cook by setting out the right balance between saturated fats and unsaturated fats, but each recipe details its nutritional composition. For those concerned about keeping their cholesterol levels low, this book is a valuable asset.

Not all high fat foods should be avoided equally: oily fish has a special place in the diet and is universally recommended once a week, and following a heart attack, health professionals advise eating 2–4 portions of oily fish every week, or a supplement containing 1g daily of the omega 3 oils, DHA and EPA for up to 4 years.

While nuts are considered high in fats, what many people do not know is that they are also cardio-protective. This is because of the range of nutrients that they provide, including the heart-healthy monounsaturated fatty acids, naturally occurring plant sterols, vegetable fiber, vitamin E, magnesium, potassium, and other plant substances. So while it is important to avoid an excessive intake of nuts, they can still be incorporated into recipes, and used as snacks as part of a low fat approach to eating.

At HEART UK we are passionate about preventing premature deaths caused by high cholesterol and cardiovascular disease. We also work to raise awareness about the risks of high cholesterol, lobby for better detection of those at risk, and support health professional training. It's also why we work with a variety of partners to promote healthier lifestyle options.

We are always delighted to hear from people with high cholesterol and their families, and we can provide advice and support via our helpline (www.heartuk.org.uk). One of the things we get asked for most are ideas for healthy meals and snacks to help lower cholesterol. Having picked up this book, we hope you share our enthusiasm for it, and we hope you get pleasure from making and sharing these recipes with friends.

Jules Payne
Chief Executive
HEART UK – The Cholesterol Charity

Introduction

For me to write a low-fat cookbook is a bit like having only two peas in a pod, as fat is important to chefs. We tell everyone that fat is where the flavor comes from; we love butter, cream, pork fat, beef fat, dripping, cracklings, chicken skin, and bacon—don't tell me you don't too! Unfortunately, flavorsome as these fats all are, they have a nasty habit of clogging up your pipes and contain a high amount of calories which don't flatter the waistband.

So why am I writing a low-fat cookbook? Well, to be honest, I'm in the healthy groove, having written five books geared toward people with diabetes, I love to prove that you can diet, and still enjoy your food. I'm not a health messiah, but I do intend over the next few years to tackle many of the problem eating areas that plague us all. I enjoy being challenged; how do you cook lovely food when you can't use the chefs' favorite ingredient, fat?

So I've done my world tour, looked at all the dishes I enjoy eating, and then analysed them to see if they can enter the low-fat zone. Some dishes couldn't, and hit the cutting-room floor, but many could, as with the addition of one or two spices or herbs, you can more than compensate for the flavor lost through omitting fat.

I have to be honest, I don't necessarily think the establishment has got it all right in the omission of all fats—there are good fats and there are bad fats—but I've been a good lad and done just that. I still hanker after the day the medical experts tell us that we don't have to cut back too stringently on that avocado, olive, and canola oil, and that it's okay to eat high-fat fish, as we know they are very good for the heart.

But I'm sure you're not interested in my fantasies! You've been told by your doc that all fat must go, and that's the reason you're thumbing through this book. But it's *you* who has to decide what food style suits you best; you must work out an eating plan that you can achieve, and by using the recipes in this book, I hope you'll realize that even if you've been put on a strict regime by your doctor, you can still look forward to each meal.

I've read the books, seen the movie, and worn the T-shirt, and so many recipes that stick to the rules can only be described as disappointing. Let me try and change all that by giving you a diverse collection of low-fat recipes from around the world. You'll recognize many of the recipe names—cooking isn't rocket science after all, it's a rubber ball that comes bouncing back to home; it's been done before, but I hope I've added that little *je ne sais quoi* which makes my dishes jump off the pages of this book, and into your psyche.

I've had fun writing this book; my pen has flowed with enjoyment and I'll tell you something, I feel better for it, and I've lost loads of weight as a side effect, so that can't be bad.

Now back to that treadmill . . .

Antony Worrall Thompson

Low-fat low-down

by Juliette Kellow BSc RD

Think of a low-fat diet and, for many of us, that instantly conjures up images of bland, boring food that we derive little pleasure from eating. It's a diet we choose simply because it's "good for us", when in reality we'd much rather be munching our way through a mouth-watering plate of creamy pasta or a juicy pan-fried steak.

Well, congratulations on picking up this book! Whether you want to lose weight, look after your heart, eat more healthily, or follow a low-fat diet to help you with a specific health problem, we guarantee that *The Essential Low Fat Cookbook* is for you. It's packed with delicious recipes that you'll actually want to cook and eat. Better still, your taste buds won't even realize that what you're eating is low in fat.

We've provided detailed nutrition information per serving for every single recipe in this book, including calories, fat, saturates, sugars, salt, and fiber. Plus, we've provided the nutrition information for fat per 3½ oz. We've followed in the footsteps of food companies and decided to use the same definition of "low-fat" as supermarkets and manufacturers. That helps to make it less confusing for you—and means that every recipe in this book contains 3g fat or less per 3½ oz.

Eating a diet that contains too much saturated fat is a real problem in the Western world, which is sadly reflected in a range of associated health problems, including heart disease and obesity, two major diseases that are well established as causing premature death. It's no surprise that health professionals recommend cutting back on the amount of fat we consume.

But eating the low-fat way isn't just great for shifting excess pounds, and helping to keep the heart healthy. A low-fat diet can also help to reduce the risk of insulin resistance, a condition that's often a warning sign for Type 2 diabetes. Meanwhile, low-fat diets can be used as part of a treatment program for a variety of health conditions, such as gallstones or gall bladder disease.

Many of us struggle to stick to a low-fat way of eating though, usually because we get bored of the same old low-fat ingredients day in, day out. Bizarrely, some of us even go as far as choosing foods we don't like that much, making mealtimes even more of a penance than a pleasure. And then, we have a tendency to be unimaginative when it comes to preparing these ingredients. It's no surprise that a diet consisting of little other than grilled chicken or fish, salads, and baked potatoes with cottage cheese quickly turns off our taste buds, and leaves us craving a huge plate of hamburger and french fries or fried chicken with rice and beans.

That's where *The Essential Low Fat Cookbook* comes to the rescue. Sure, fat adds flavor to food, but armed with a few tips and tricks—and a handful of staple, flavorsome ingredients in your kitchen—it's easy to turn even the plainest chicken breast, or piece of cod into a culinary delight, without drowning it in oil, butter, or cream. Better still, you don't need to give up red meat, cheese, and eggs—or even desserts and cakes for that matter. As you turn the pages, chances are you'll be delighted to find that many of your long-held beliefs about low-fat diets, are actually nothing more than myths.

Why a low-fat diet?

Scientific studies show that having too much fat, particularly saturated fat, in our diets is associated with a long list of health problems. The good news is that health experts agree that cutting down on fat by following a low-fat diet, can help to reduce our risk of many of these conditions.

Keep your heart healthy

Without doubt, cardiovascular disease (CVD)—which includes all the diseases of the heart and circulatory system—is the one condition everyone links to diets high in saturated fat. With good reason. According to the World Health Organization, in 2005, no less than 17.5 million people died of the condition, accounting for 30 percent of all deaths throughout the world.

In the UK, statistics from the British Heart Foundation reveal that CVD is the number one killer, responsible for a staggering 35 percent of all deaths. About half of these are from coronary heart disease (which includes heart attacks and angina), and another quarter from strokes. It's an even grimmer picture for other European countries. Data from European Cardiovascular Disease Statistics shows that CVD causes 38 percent of deaths in Norway, 40 percent in Germany, and a staggering 48 percent in Greece, despite the commonly held belief that a Mediterranean diet is good for the heart. Even France, which is often highlighted as having much lower rates of CVD, sees 29 percent of its population dying from the condition. In total, 48 percent of deaths in Europe are caused by the condition.

It's a similar picture throughout the Western world. In Canada, 32 percent of people die from CVD. In America, the incidence stands at 37 percent. Meanwhile, on the other side of the world, just over a third of Australians die from the condition, while in New Zealand, it jumps to 40 percent.

It's well established that many factors are linked to an increased risk of cardiovascular disease, including things that we can't change, such as being male, having a family history of the condition (especially where family members have a heart attack, angina, or die from heart disease before the age of 55 in a man or 65 in a woman), being of South Asian origin, and simply getting older. There are also many risk factors that we can alter, such as not smoking, and being more active. That's where changing our eating habits comes into play. It's widely accepted that diets high in fat, particularly saturated fat—the type found predominantly in foods such as butter, lard, hard margarines, ghee, full-fat dairy products, and meat—have a part to play in the development of CVD.

In particular, high intakes of fat (especially saturates), increase blood cholesterol, which is one of the major risk factors for coronary heart disease. It's something most of us need to worry about, too, even if we're female—it's a total myth that only men suffer from high cholesterol. Figures from the American Heart Association reveal that 47.7 million men, and 54.5 million women in the United States have high cholesterol. The solution: cut down on fat to reduce your risk of high cholesterol, which in turn eliminates one of the risk factors for the number one killer disease. And over the course of this book, we'll show you just how to do that.

Stay slim

Unless you've been living on Mars for the last decade, it probably comes as no surprise to learn that obesity is a major health problem in the Western world. According to the World Health Organization (WHO), currently more than 1 billion adults around the world are overweight, and at least 300 million of them are clinically obese.

In the US, 67 percent of adults have a weight problem, while in Canada, it's 59 percent, and in the UK 61 percent. Within Europe, Italy has one of the lowest incidences of weight problems, although 44 percent of the population are still classified as overweight or obese. This rises to 49 percent in France, 57 percent in Greece, and 67 percent in Germany. The picture is just as bad in the Southern

Hemisphere, where 49 percent of Australians, 63 percent of New Zealanders, and 45 percent of South Africans are too heavy. Meanwhile, even those countries with no tradition of weight problems are now seeing the incidence rise: 19 percent of Chinese, 23 percent of Japanese, 32 percent of Thais, and 41 percent of Brazilians are now overweight or obese. You get the picture.

Expanding waistlines come with an extensive list of health problems, including raised blood pressure and cholesterol, both of which are risk factors for CVD. Being overweight, even by a small amount, dramatically increases the risk of Type 2 diabetes, too—in fact, the World Health Organization believes that nine out of 10 people with the condition are overweight or obese. Then there's the increased risk of a range of cancers (see right). Overweight and obese adults are also more likely to suffer with gallstones, osteoarthritis, breathing difficulties, skin problems, infertility, sleep disturbances, and mental health problems such as depression.

The question of whether it's simply fat that makes us fat has been debated by scientists for years. We know for sure that excessive weight gain occurs when our energy (or calorie) intake from food and drink exceeds the amount of energy (or calories) that we burn off. As a result, most experts agree that no one food, nutrient, or group of foods makes us fat. It's our overall calorie intake that dictates whether we end up loosening or tightening our belts.

Nevertheless, fat can have a dramatic effect on that calorie content. Fat is a concentrated source of energy, providing nine calories per gram—twice as many as the same amount of protein or carbohydrate. As a result, foods that contain a lot of fat, also tend to be high in calories. And when we regularly take in too many calories, the pounds start to pile on.

Meanwhile, despite adding calories, fat adds very little actual quantity to our diet. This may be important as research shows that it's the actual quantity of food that we eat that helps to fill us up and make us feel satisfied. For example, 200g of mashed potatoes contain 144 calories and 0.2g fat. Add 15g butter and that portion of potatoes (which now weighs just 15g more) provides 255 calories and 12.5g fat. The reality: we've added 8 percent more food, but a massive 44 percent more calories.

Other research shows that fat seems to have a less satiating or filling effect than other food components such as protein and fiber, with the result that when we have a high-fat diet, it's harder to satisfy hunger, so we end up eating more. Then there's the effect that fat has on our taste buds. Undoubtedly, it helps to make food taste good—especially when it's combined with sugar, processed carbs, or salt—so that we're more likely to overeat.

The reality: when we eat a high-fat diet, it's easy to consume a large number of calories—and if we don't burn these off, we risk becoming obese, and suffering a range of health problems. So cutting down on fat (especially saturated fat), makes sense if we want to control our weight, or lose excess pounds.

Myth makeover

The myth: Low-fat and fat-free foods are low in calories.

The makeover: Foods that are described as "low-fat" or "fat-free" aren't automatically low in calories or calorie-free. In fact, some low-fat products may actually be higher in calories than standard products, thanks to them containing extra sugars and thickeners to boost the flavor and texture. Some people also mistakenly believe that they can eat more if they're choosing low-fat products. But this is rarely the case. In reality, two low-fat cookies, for example, will probably contain more calories than one standard cookie.

Protect yourself from cancer

An excess of body fat is one of the greatest risk factors for many cancers. According to the World Cancer Research Fund, excessive body fat increases the risk of cancers of the esophagus, pancreas, bowel, endometrium, kidney, and breast, and probably also puts us at risk for cancers of the gall bladder and liver.

The World Cancer Research Fund also reveals that high-fat diets themselves—regardless of weight—are linked to an increased risk of lung cancer, the most common type in the world, making up 13 percent of all cancers. High-fat diets are also linked to breast cancer, the most common cancer in women, especially post-menopausal breast cancer. Meanwhile, foods containing animal fat may contribute to an increased risk of colorectal or bowel cancer, representing a tenth of all cancers globally. So cut down on fat, and you also help to lower your chances of developing certain cancers.

Fight insulin resistance

Obesity is one of the major risk factors for insulin resistance. However, scientists are discovering increasingly that high fat intakes, particularly of saturated fats, are linked to insulin resistance, independently of body weight. In contrast, polyunsaturated fats and monounsaturated fats seem to improve insulin sensitivity.

The problem with insulin resistance is that it's a forerunner of Type 2 diabetes—a condition that's becoming increasingly common in Western countries. In this condition, the body's cells don't respond properly to the insulin produced by the pancreas; in other words, the cells are resistant to the effects of insulin, a hormone that regulates blood sugar levels. As a result, the pancreas continues to pump out more and more insulin to keep blood sugar levels within normal limits. Eventually the pancreas fails to keep up with this increased demand for insulin, so blood sugar levels rise, and the stage is set for Type 2 diabetes.

The link between high fat intakes and insulin resistance is an area of science that needs more research, but inevitably it seems that cutting back on fat may help to lower the chances of insulin resistance and Type 2 diabetes.

Guard against gallstones

Being overweight increases the risk of gallstones—and the more overweight you are, the more the risk rises. According to the National Institute of Diabetes and Digestive and Kidney Disease, however, high-fat diets may also make a person more susceptible to them.

Gallstones are small stones that form in the gall bladder or its ducts. They occur when bile—which helps to digest fats—forms stones made from, among other things, hardened cholesterol-like material (this has nothing to do with cholesterol levels in the blood). Bile is made in the liver, then passes through a series of "passageways" called bile ducts, into the gall bladder, where it is stored. The gall bladder then releases bile into the digestive system whenever it's needed to digest fat.

Although it's still an area that's being researched, it's thought that high-fat diets increase the risk of gallstones, because the liver produces bile with a higher cholesterol content. The cholesterol begins to form small crystals, which then join together to form stones.

Gallstones often don't cause any symptoms, but if they get trapped in the bile ducts, they can prevent the normal flow of bile, which results in sporadic abdominal pain. In severe cases, gallstones can trigger inflammation of the gall bladder, known as cholecystitis, resulting in symptoms such as a fever, constant stomach pains, and even jaundice.

Health professionals agree that losing weight is one of the best things you can do to reduce the risk of developing gallstones, and ease symptoms if you already have them. But it's important to do this slowly, as rapid weight loss—more than two to three pounds per week—is actually associated with a greater risk of gallstones. This is because during crash diets, when body fat is broken down to supply energy, extra cholesterol is released into the bile. Indeed, people who follow very low-calorie diets, or have weight-loss surgery, are at high risk of gallstones.

Eating a low-fat diet can also help to ease the symptoms of gallstones (though the only way you can actually get rid of them is to have surgery). Unsurprisingly, pain caused by gallstones often comes after eating a fatty meal, when the gall bladder needs to release bile to digest the fat. Therefore, a lower-fat diet means that less bile is needed, so the gall bladder doesn't need to work as hard.

Get a better night's sleep

Believe it or not, a few studies show that high fat intakes, especially during the evening, may disrupt our sleep patterns. One small Brazilian study, for example, found that when volunteers had a high fat intake throughout the day, or just a high-fat dinner, they woke more frequently during the night as a result of tossing and turning, were more likely to suffer with abnormal breathing while sleeping, and spent less time in REM sleep—the type of sleep that helps to really rest and restore the body.

In another study from the University of Arizona, women who had high intakes of fat and saturates were far more likely to suffer with breathing disorders while they were sleeping, regardless of their weight. In fact, they consumed 28g more fat a day than those women who didn't suffer with sleep disturbances. Whether it's sleep disturbance that results in a higher intake of fat the next day, or a high-fat diet that causes poorer sleep, remains unclear. It's certainly an area that needs a lot more research before any definitive conclusions can be made. But if you have trouble sleeping, it certainly won't do any harm to cut down on fat, and see if it makes a difference.

Breathe easy

It may not seem like an obvious link, but scientists are increasingly discovering that high-fat diets may aggravate the symptoms of asthma, and may also make asthma medication less effective. In a recent Australian study, researchers discovered that asthma sufferers who ate a burger and fries containing 60g fat had lungs that were more inflamed than asthma sufferers who ate a low-fat yogurt containing just 3g fat. Treatment for asthma was also less effective in the burger eaters.

In another study, this time from Spain, increased intakes of saturated fats, and particularly butter, were linked to asthma in children. Yet more research from Kansas State University looked at the effect of a high-fat meal on lung function, and concluded that high-fat diets may contribute to chronic inflammatory diseases of the airway and lungs.

The link between fat intakes and breathing is another relatively new area of research, and many more large-scale studies need to be carried out before any definite conclusions can be made. But early investigations certainly seem to link high-fat intakes with breathing difficulties.

Treat health problems

Diets that are low in saturated fat are recommended to treat a range of health problems, including high cholesterol and obesity, or as part of the dietary treatment for insulin resistance, Type 2 diabetes, and gallstones, frequently in combination with losing weight, if necessary.

Low-fat diets are usually also advised for people who have had surgery for weight loss such as gastric bands or bypasses, although it's important that anyone who's about to undergo, or who has had such a procedure, follows the specific advice of their consultant. Meanwhile, low-fat diets are often recommended to treat a range of other complaints, including some digestive disorders, but again, the advice of a doctor or dietitian should always be followed.

Getting to grips with the guidelines

Advice on the maximum amount of fat we should eat varies from country to country. Generally speaking, in developed countries, it's based on preventing chronic diseases such as heart disease.

Most health agencies around the world express their recommendations for maximum fat intakes as a percentage of calories that should come from fat rather than an actual number of grams of fat. This may seem complicated, but it's done this way because not everyone has the same calorie needs—for example, men tend to need more calories than women because they are physically bigger. Using these percentage guidelines, health professionals can then work out suitable fat intakes for different groups of people—and provide advice on the maximum grams of fat they should aim for.

To prevent cardiovascular disease, most health agencies recommend that no more than a third of our calories come from fat, and no more than one tenth from saturates.

Some countries also recommend a lower limit to help ensure that populations don't have intakes that are so low, they fail to get enough calories, healthy fats, or fat-soluble vitamins. In America, for example, while the upper limit is set at 35 percent of calories from fat, and 10 percent from saturates, the United States Department of Agriculture also recommends that no fewer than 20 percent of calories come from fat. In Australia and New Zealand, the recommendations are the same.

On a global level, the World Health Organization recommends no fewer than 15 percent of calories come from fat, although women of reproductive age and underweight adults should have no fewer than 20 percent. At the other end of the scale, the WHO confirms that most people should get no more than 30–35 percent of calories from fat.

But while there are clear guidelines as to the maximum amount of fat we should eat to prevent chronic diseases, and the minimum amount to ensure that we get all the nutrients we need, surprisingly, there are no clear guidelines to identify what actually constitutes a low-fat diet.

When it comes to research, most clinical trials seem to classify a low-fat diet as one in which fat provides anything from 20–30 percent of calories. Indeed, in weight-loss trials, a fat restriction in this range seems to be more effective at shifting the pounds than a very low fat intake, where fat provides fewer than 20 percent of calories. This is probably because diets that are extremely low in fat, tend to be too restrictive and boring for most people, with the result that they give up easily. Furthermore, research shows that overweight people who have 20–30 percent of their calories from fat, are more likely to keep the weight off in the long term.

So, if most health experts agree that a low-fat diet is one where around 20–30 percent of calories come from fat, what does this mean in practice? The table overleaf shows the maximum number of grams of fat to aim for, depending on different calorie intakes.

Daily calorie intake	Recommended intake of fat grams where...		
	...20% of calories come from fat	...25% of calories come from fat	...30% of calories come from fat
1,250	28	35	42
1,500	33	42	50
1,750	39	49	58
2,000	44	56	67
2,250	50	63	75
2,500	56	69	83

A word about the under-5s

It's important to encourage good eating habits in children as soon as possible. However, health experts agree that low-fat diets are unsuitable for most children under the age of five, because they can provide insufficient calories and nutrients for growth. Because young children only have small tummies, they don't physically have room to eat large amounts. This means that meals and snacks need to be packed with calories and nutrients. Fat can make an important contribution to these calorie needs, as well as providing essential fatty acids and fat-soluble vitamins.

That's not to say children should be given high-fat, nutrient-poor foods such as chocolate, cookies, and cakes to boost their calorie intake. Instead, they should get their fat and calories from nutrient-rich foods such as whole milk (children under the age of two shouldn't be given skim, 1% or reduced fat milk), meat, eggs, cheese, and oil-rich fish. As children approach school age, they should gradually move toward eating a diet that's based on healthy eating guidelines, and, by the age of five, their diet should be low in fat, sugar, and salt, and high in fiber, with five fruits and vegetables a day—just like adults.

Percent Daily Values

To help people make sense of the nutrition information on food packs and put it in the context of their own diet, many manufacturers now label their products with Daily Values (DVs). These are based on dietary requirements for a daily 2,000 calorie allowance and certain nutrients needed for a balanced, healthy diet. DVs for total fat, saturated fat, cholesterol, and sodium are maximum amounts, so it doesn't matter if less than this is consumed (bear in mind that DVs for fat are based on preventing disease, rather than meeting the requirements of a low-fat diet). Others, for example for total carbohydrate and dietary fiber represent the minimum amounts recommended and means you should consume at least this amount per day.

Quite simply, the amount of a nutrient contained within a typical serving of the food is compared to the DV, and then expressed as a percentage. For example, 18% for total fat means that one serving furnishes 18% of the total amount of fat that you could eat in a day and stay within public health recommendations.

The %DV gives you a framework for deciding if a food is high or low in a nutrient. Use the Quick Guide to %DV: 5% or less is low and 20% or more is high.

Percent Daily Values		
Calories	2,000	2,500
Total Fat (g)	65	80
Saturated Fat (g)	20	25
Cholesterol (mg)	300	300
Sodium (mg)	2,400	2,400
Total Carbohydrate (g)	300	375
Dietary Fiber	25	30

So how much fat are we eating?

While there is no doubt in the Western world that most people eat too much fat, particularly saturates, the good news is that values have been dropping gradually over the past decade. The UK is a prime example. Figures from the National Diet and Nutrition Survey published in 2001, revealed that adults were getting 33.3 percent of their calories from fat. The most recent survey published in 2010, found this figure had dropped to 32.9 percent, just within current guidelines. Nevertheless, intakes of saturates remain too high, with adults currently getting 12 percent of their calories from this nutrient, compared to the recommended maximum of 10 percent.

Sadly, the figures are less encouraging for children and teenagers. While fat intakes have certainly dropped in the past decade, on average, boys still currently get 34 percent of their calories from fat, and girls 35.2 percent—considerably more than the recommended maximum of 33 percent. Saturated fat intakes are even more of a problem, with children and teenagers having, on average, about 13 percent of their calories from this nutrient.

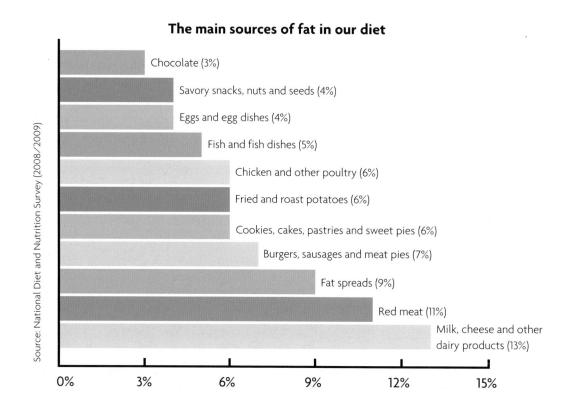

The main sources of fat in our diet

Source: National Diet and Nutrition Survey (2008/2009)

- Chocolate (3%)
- Savory snacks, nuts and seeds (4%)
- Eggs and egg dishes (4%)
- Fish and fish dishes (5%)
- Chicken and other poultry (6%)
- Fried and roast potatoes (6%)
- Cookies, cakes, pastries and sweet pies (6%)
- Burgers, sausages and meat pies (7%)
- Fat spreads (9%)
- Red meat (11%)
- Milk, cheese and other dairy products (13%)

0% 3% 6% 9% 12% 15%

Myth makeover

The myth: A fat-free diet is even better than a low-fat diet.

The makeover: It's difficult to follow a fat-free diet since most foods, even fruit and vegetables, provide small amounts of fat. Meanwhile, we actually need some fat in our diet. Fat helps to insulate the body, and small amounts around the major organs help to protect them. Certain components of fat are also important for making hormones, and are an essential part of our cells. Plus, fat-soluble vitamins A, D, E, and K are mainly found in foods that contain fat. Furthermore, two fatty acids—linoleic acid and alpha-linolenic acid—can't be made by the body and so must be supplied in the diet. Known as essential fatty acids, these are needed in small amounts for growth, healthy skin, and to protect against certain diseases. Ultimately, a fat-free diet equals a very low intake of fat-soluble vitamins and essential fats. The truth is that a fat-free diet is simply not palatable, so most people find it impossible to follow in the long term. It's good news then that it's better to opt for low-fat, than to go fat-free.

Eating the right type of fat

Even low-fat diets should still provide sufficient fat to make up 20–30 percent of calories—that's anywhere between 44g and 67g fat for a woman, and anywhere between 56g and 83g fat for a man. That's still a significant amount, so it's important that you choose healthier fats.

There are three main types of fat in food—saturates, monounsaturates, and polyunsaturates. Most foods contain a mixture of these, but are generally classified according to the type of fat found in the largest amount. In addition, some foods contain trans fats.

Eating healthily is not only about watching your total fat intake, it's also about the balance of fats in your diet. As a first step, cutting back on saturated fat is the best way to limit total fat intake. The next step would be to swap some of the saturated fat in your diet for healthier fats, such as those from mono- and polyunsaturated sources. This is vital as foods rich in these unsaturated fats help to protect us from conditions such as heart disease and diabetes. Here's the low-down...

Saturated fats

A diet high in saturates is proven to increase levels of LDL or "bad" cholesterol in the blood, one of the risk factors for heart disease. That's why health experts recommend eating fewer foods that are rich in saturates, such as fatty meats, full-fat dairy products, butter, lard, cream, cheese, and many processed foods and takeouts.

Polyunsaturated fats

Polyunsaturated fats are divided into two groups—omega-3 fats and omega-6 fats.

Omega-3 fats are divided into short- and long-chain types, both of which help to lower levels of LDL. Short-chain omega-3 fats are found in flaxseed, canola oil, walnuts, and green, leafy vegetables. The body converts short-chain omega-3s into long-chain omega-3s, but this conversion process isn't very efficient. In contrast, oil-rich fish such as mackerel, salmon, sardines, trout, herring, and fresh tuna, is a naturally rich source of "ready-made" long-chain omega-3 fats—and it's particularly these types of omega-3s that are linked to keeping the heart beating regularly, making the blood less sticky, so that blood clots are less likely, and lowering levels of triglycerides (a type of blood fat).

Omega-6 fats are found in pure vegetable oils and spreads such as sunflower, corn, grapeseed, and soy oils and margarines, as well as nuts and seeds. These fats lower "bad" cholesterol, but also slightly increase levels of HDL or "good" cholesterol, the type that helps to protect against heart disease.

Monounsaturated fats

These have a double-whammy effect on cholesterol levels. As well as lowering LDL cholesterol, they also raise HDL cholesterol. Good sources include olive oil, canola oil, avocados, nuts, and seeds.

Trans fats

Trans fats are created from hydrogenated fats or hydrogenated vegetable oils, which are sometimes used as an ingredient in processed foods in order to extend their shelf life. They're even more harmful to heart health than saturates, because as well as increasing LDL cholesterol, they also lower HDL cholesterol. In America, products are labeled with the amount of trans fats they contain, but in the UK, this is uncommon. To see if a food contains trans fats, you need to look at the ingredients. If a product contains hydrogenated vegetable fat or oil as an ingredient, it will almost certainly contain trans fats— and the higher up the list the ingredient appears, the more trans fats the product will contain. In general, hydrogenated vegetable fats and oils are found in cakes, cookies, margarines, takeouts, pastry, pies, and fried foods—although in the US there's good news as many manufacturers have removed them from their products.

Choosing a low-fat diet

Over the following pages, you'll find lots more detail on the best foods to choose (and avoid), to help you stick to a low-fat diet. Nevertheless, looking at food labels is one of the easiest ways to identify whether or not a food contains a little, or a lot of fat. Any food that contains 3g fat or less per 3½ oz is low in fat. Products with 20g fat or more in 3½ oz, are high in fat.

Be a supermarket sleuth

As well as providing detailed nutrition information, many products also include additional information on the packaging to help us make healthier choices. Here's what some of these claims mean (manufacturers have to abide by these definitions by law, so you can be confident claims are correct if they appear on a product):

- Low-fat—foods must contain 3g of fat or less per 3½ oz, while fluids must contain 1.5g fat or less per 1/3 cup (the exception is 1.8g fat per 1/3 cup for reduced fat milk).
- Fat-free—foods or fluids must contain 0.5g of fat or less per 3½ oz, or per 1/3 cup.
- Reduced fat—the food must contain 30 percent less fat than a similar standard product. This doesn't mean the product is low-fat though!
- Low saturates—the total of the saturated fat and trans fats in the product must be 1.5g or less per 3½ oz for food, and 0.75g per 1/3 cup for fluid.
- Saturates-free—the total of the saturated fat and trans fats in the product must be 0.1g or less per 3½ oz, or per 1/3 cup.
- Light or Lite—this has to follow the same rules as "reduced" and the product must outline the characteristics that make it light or lite, for example, a reduction in fat or saturates.

Your essential guide to cutting down on fat

Red meat

Red meat has come under attack in the past few decades for its high fat—and particularly saturated fat content, and it's easy to see why. According to the most recent National Diet and Nutrition Survey, red meat provides 11 percent of the fat in our diet, with burgers, sausages, and pies providing an extra 7 percent. The good news is that you don't have to give up red meat altogether to follow a low-fat diet—and yes, you did read that correctly!

Thanks to modern feeding programmes, which breed leaner animals, and new butchery techniques that remove more fat, red meat is now leaner than it's ever been. For example, the fat content of pork has dropped from 30 percent in the 1950s to just 4 percent today. Meanwhile, lean beef is now as low as 5 percent fat, and lamb, 8 percent fat.

Better still, while most of us think that red meat is packed with artery-clogging saturates, around half the fat is actually heart-healthy monounsaturates, particularly oleic acid—the same type of fat found in olive oil.

As a result, it's easier than ever to continue enjoying red meat, while keeping fat intakes down. Nevertheless, it's important to choose cuts wisely. For example, while lean pork is just 4 percent fat, belly pork contains five times that amount. Similarly, lean beef is just 5 percent fat, but typical ground meat is 16 percent fat. The golden rule is to look at the nutrition information on the packaging before buying—and if you prefer to buy from a butcher, get him to trim as much fat off as possible. Then don't go and ruin all your hard work by cooking it in loads of oil—opt for low-fat cooking methods instead.

Meat products such as sausages, bacon and cured meats, are generally all much higher in fat (and also salt) than fresh meat, so it's wise to steer clear of these. The one exception is cooked ham, which often has the lowest fat content of all popular meats, although it's still high in salt.

If you would like a change from beef, lamb, or pork, veal and game, such as venison, both contain less than 2 percent fat, and so are excellent choices. Rabbit, with just under 6 percent fat, contains slightly more fat than lean beef.

It's also important to control portions. Many of us continue to eat large amounts of red meat—often double the amount health experts recommend. In fact, a suitable portion of meat should fit into the palm of your hand, or be the same size as a pack of cards.

Cut the fat

Tips for enjoying red meat

- Choose the leanest cuts of meat you can find —most pre-packed meat these days includes nutrition information, so check the fat content before putting it in your cart.
- If you buy meat from a butcher, ask for it to be trimmed to remove any visible fat. Or for pre-packed meat, trim it yourself—this is particularly important if you love the fat on bacon, or a pork chop. If it's not there, you won't be tempted to eat it!
- Make lean pork your meat of choice—it contains less fat than beef or lamb.
- Try venison or veal for a change—but don't add loads of fat to cook them.
- Go for trimmed Canadian bacon, which is around 7 percent fat, rather than streaky bacon with 24 percent fat!
- Check the fat content of ground beef before you buy—it can vary dramatically from around 5 percent fat, for extra lean meat, up to 17 percent fat for ordinary ground beef.
- Cut back on portion sizes—around 3½ oz per person is more than enough—and add extra vegetables or beans to boost the quantity of food on your plate.
- Don't add extra fat to meat when you cook it—investing in a decent nonstick frying pan or wok means you will be able to cook many types of meat without the need for oil.

- Use cooking methods that don't require fat, such as broiling, grilling, baking, casseroling or pot roasting.
- Marinate lean meat before cooking it to add flavor, and keep it moist while it cooks.
- Avoid the need to "seal" a meat roast (when it's fried in oil before roasting) by placing it into a very hot preheated oven for 15 minutes at the start of cooking. The high temperature will "seal" the meat without you having to add any oil. Then, after 15 minutes, turn the oven temperature down to your regular cooking temperature.
- Don't be fooled into thinking that premium sausages are lower in fat—they're often bigger and contain more meat than cheaper varieties, so actually have more fat. Even reduced-fat sausages usually contain significant amounts of fat. For example, a premium sausage can contain 11g fat, while an ordinary sausage contains 8g fat, and a reduced-fat sausage 6g fat.
- Skip cured meats such as chorizo, bologna, salami, pepperoni, and mortadella—all the little white blobs you can see are fat. Chorizo, for example, can easily contain more than 40 percent fat, while salami usually contains in excess of 30 percent fat.
- Ham can be a good choice for including in a low-fat diet, but it's important to choose carefully. Many cooked hams can contain as little as 3 percent fat. Proscuitto, on the other hand, may contain 15 percent.

Poultry

Chicken and turkey are both thought of as lower-fat alternatives to red meat—and indeed they can be. However, a study conducted by the Institute of Brain Chemistry and Human Nutrition at London Metropolitan University in 2005, found that chicken has got fattier in the past 35 years: in 1970, a chicken was found to contain around 9 percent fat, compared with 23 percent fat in 2005. The reason, scientists believe, is that chickens roam less, and are given artificial feed. Even organic chickens, which have more room to move about, but still don't have to search for their own food, were found to contain 17 percent fat.

So, with this in mind, when it comes to selecting poultry, it's just as important to choose as wisely as you would with red meat. The most important rule is to cook poultry without the skin, remove any visible fat, and avoid cooking with extra fat. But you can also cut down on fat further by opting for the white breast meat, rather than the darker meat—raw chicken breast contains just 1 percent fat, whereas dark meat contains just under 3 percent fat.

Meanwhile, don't be tempted to choose duck or goose instead—both are very fatty. Duck, for example, contains six times more fat than chicken breast.

8 smart swaps				
Swap this	g fat	For this	g fat	Save this amount of fat
1 broiled slice of bacon (20g)	5g	1 broiled lean slice of Canadian bacon (25g)	3g	2g
3½ oz raw ordinary ground beef	16g	3½ oz extra-lean ground beef	10g	6g
1 broiled premium sausage (50g)	11g	1 broiled reduced-fat sausage (40g)	6g	5g
3½ oz lean roast leg of lamb, well done*	9g	3½ oz lean roast leg of pork, well done*	5g	4g
3½ oz raw dark turkey meat	3g	3½ oz raw turkey breast	1g	2g
125g broiled sirloin steak, well done*	12g	125g broiled round steak	7g	5g
4 small thin slices salami (20g)	8g	1 slice lean ham (23g)	1g	7g
1 roasted chicken leg quarter with skin (190g)	32g	1 broiled skinless chicken breast (130g)	3g	29g

*The longer you cook meat, the more fat drips out, so well done usually has less fat than rare.

Fish

Health experts recommend that we eat two portions of fish each week, one of which should be an oil-rich fish such as salmon, mackerel, sardines, or trout. But they don't recommend that you eat it smothered in batter, and fried in oil! All white fish and shellfish such as crab, shrimp, and mussels tend to be great low-fat options, but, as the name suggests, oil-rich fish are much higher in fat. The good news is, as we've already mentioned, oil-rich fish contain heart-healthy omega-3 fats, so it's important to include these types of fish, even when you're cutting down on the total amount of fat in your diet.

What's most important is how you cook fish. Serve a 3½ oz fillet of baked cod, and you'll have just 1g fat. But take that same piece of cod, dip it in batter then pop it into the deep fat fryer, and you'll have 15g fat! Fortunately, fish lends itself to many low-fat cooking methods including baking, broiling, steaming and poaching, so it's easy to add variety to your meals.

Meanwhile, if you're a fan of canned fish, opting for varieties in spring water rather than oil will keep the fat content down—canned tuna in oil, for example, contains 15 times more fat than canned tuna in water!

As for processed products such as ready-prepared breaded or battered fish, fish cakes, or fish sticks, always check the nutrition information on the packaging first. Remember, only foods with 3g of fat or less per 3½ oz are considered to be low-fat products. Most breaded fish contain more than 3g fat per 3½ oz, but there are a few exceptions.

A diet rich in fish oils is particularly important following a heart attack. The American Heart Association recommends eating fatty fish at least two times (two servings) a week.

Some oil-rich fish contain more fat than others. For example, mackerel contains more fat than salmon, which in turn contains more fat than trout. Similarly, steamed salmon contains around three times more fat than canned salmon.

How much fat is in my fish? (per 3½ oz raw)

Monkfish	less than 1g	Squid	2g	Fresh tuna	5g
Shrimp	less than 1g	Plaice	2g	Rainbow trout	5g
Haddock	less than 1g	Halibut	2g	Sardines	9g
Mussels (in shells)	less than 1g	Sea bass	3g	Salmon	12g
Cod	less than 1g	Red mullet	4g	Herring	13g
Pollock	less than 1g	Brown trout	4g	Mackerel	16g
Lemon sole	1g	Swordfish	4g		
		Smoked salmon	5g		

Going for canned?

Fat content per 3½ oz (canned and drained where appropriate)

Crab in brine	less than 1g	Sardines in tomato sauce	10g
Tuna in brine	less than 1g	Sardines in oil	14g
Pink salmon in brine	7g	Herring in tomato sauce	14g
Red salmon in brine	8g	Mackerel in tomato sauce	15g
Tuna in oil	9g	Mackerel in brine	18g
Sardines in brine	10g		

Dairy and eggs

With milk, cheese, other dairy products, and eggs accounting for roughly a sixth of the fat in our diets according to the latest National Diet and Nutrition Survey, it's not surprising that these foods often come under fire. Fortunately, manufacturers have risen to the challenge set by health professionals, and have provided us with a wide range of lower-fat products. And we've certainly embraced them. In fact, we now consume almost four times more reduced fat milk than we do whole milk.

Milk

While skim and reduced fat milks have been around for several decades now, the latest addition to our supermarket shelves is 1% milk. As the name suggests, this contains just 1g fat per 100ml and is effectively a halfway option between skim milk, which is virtually fat-free, and reduced fat milk, which contains just under 2g fat per 100ml. All three options are a better alternative to whole or full-fat milk, which contains just under 4g fat per 100ml, and the good news is that all of these can be used in cooking in the same way you would use whole milk.

As for variations on a standard quart, organic and goat's milk is now widely available in fat-free, reduced fat and whole or full-fat varieties. Even lactose-free milks may come in reduced fat as well as whole varieties. Soy milk can have varying levels of fat and isn't described as fat-free or reduced fat, so check the label.

Myth makeover

The myth: Reduced fat milk contains less calcium than whole milk.
The makeover: Most people are surprised to learn that skim, 1% and reduced fat milk actually contain slightly more calcium than full fat varieties. This is because calcium is found in the watery part of the milk, and not the creamy part. As a result, when the cream is removed to cut fat, calcium intakes aren't affected.

Cheese

Cheese is generally considered to be off-limits when you're cutting down on fat, but low-fat varieties do exist. Cottage cheese, ricotta and low-fat soft cheeses are perfect for using in cooking to add a creamy texture, and for using in sandwiches and wraps in place of hard cheeses.

Tips for enjoying cheese

- A small amount of hard cheese looks like a lot more when it's grated, especially if you use the finest grating option.
- Go for extra mature Cheddar rather than mild varieties—you won't need to use as much to get the same cheesy flavor.
- Similarly, swap regular hard cheeses for blue-veined cheeses—they contain similar amounts of fat, but blue cheeses tend to have a stronger flavor so you won't need to use as much.
- Use less cheese in sauces and instead grate a little Parmesan on top of dishes—your taste buds will be fooled into thinking the dish is loaded with cheese.
- Try reduced-fat varieties of cheese—many now melt just as easily as full-fat varieties and so are perfect for cooking.
- Swap Cheddar for other varieties of cheese that are naturally lower in fat.
- Keep portions of cheese small—health experts say a piece around the size of a small matchbox (30g) counts as one portion. We should aim to have three portions of dairy a day, for example a little over ½ cup of skim milk, a small container of yogurt, and 1¼ oz of cheese.

How much fat is in my cheese? (per 3½ oz)

Many of these varieties now come in reduced-fat options so check the packaging to compare the fat content.

Quark	0g	Brie	27g	Wensleydale	32g
Cottage cheese	4g	Danish Blue	29g	Cheddar	33g
Ricotta	11g	Parmesan	30g	Roquefort	33g
Feta	20g	Emmental	30g	Red Leicester	34g
Mozzarella	20g	Gouda	31g	Blue Stilton	34g
Camembert	23g	Lancashire	31g	Cream cheese	48g
Edam	25g	Caerphilly	31g		
Goat's cheese	26g	Cheshire	31g		

What is Quark?

Quark is a soft cheese that's similar to natural fromage frais in terms of its flavor. It has the advantage of being completely fat-free, making it a great alternative to cream cheese in cooking.

Yogurt and fromage frais

Yogurt and fromage frais come in a startling number of varieties, so it can be difficult to know what to choose—but you really do need to know what to look for, because the variations in fat content can be equally startling. As a rule, you can't go wrong if you look for "fat-free" on the label—products described as this will contain virtually no fat. Products labeled as "low fat" are also a good option, as they are guaranteed to contain less than 3g fat per 3½ oz. Otherwise, it really is important to check out the nutrition information on the packaging. Greek yogurt might seem like a healthy option, but while fat-free and low-fat varieties exist, unless you check the label, you could end up with a product that contains 10 percent fat.

Flavored varieties of low-fat yogurt and fromage frais have never been more popular for a quick and easy dessert. Plain yogurt, while tasty on cereal and mixed with fresh fruit, also makes a great alternative to cream or mayo in dishes. In cold dishes such as chicken salad and dips, low-fat plain yogurt can simply be used in place of mayo. In heated dishes, however, it's best to use yogurt with a higher fat content rather than low-fat yogurt, as the small amount of fat helps to keep it stable and stops it from separating. Even with a higher fat content, it's still a far better option than cream—a ¾ cup container of whole milk plain yogurt contains around 5g fat, whereas the same quantity of light cream contains 27–45g fat and heavy cream can contain 45–60g fat, or more.

How to use yogurt in sauces

Start by making sure that the sauce is quite well reduced, because adding yogurt will make it watery again (unlike cream, which thickens the longer you leave it). Then add one teaspoonful of cornstarch to a ¾ cup container of whole milk plain yogurt—this will help to prevent the yogurt from separating once it's heated, and will also thicken the sauce slightly.

Take the pan off the heat, and leave to cool very slightly, then gradually beat the yogurt into the sauce a tablespoon at a time. Return to low heat, and bring the pan to a gentle simmer for one to two minutes to cook the cornstarch, and thicken the sauce. Perfect for stroganoff, pasta sauces and creamy curries.

Eggs

Depending on size, an egg contains around 6–7g of fat, so it's not exactly a low-fat product. But that's not to say that eggs can't be enjoyed as part of a nutritious, low-fat diet. Eggs lend themselves to plenty of different low-fat cooking methods such as poaching, boiling, baking, and scrambling, so there's really no need to add extra fat to them. Meanwhile, when it comes to using eggs in cooking, there's an easy way to cheat to lower the fat content. All the fat is in the yolk, while the egg white is actually fat-free. This means that it's easy to reduce the fat content of baked dishes and omelets by replacing some of the whole eggs with egg whites. Hollywood celebs may go all the way and have omelets made totally from the whites (and there is a recipe for this on page 40), but to keep the consistency and taste, it's usually better to include some whole eggs. As a general rule, swap one whole egg for two whites. So, for example, if a cake requires three whole eggs, replace this with one whole egg and four egg whites to save around 13g fat.

Myth makeover

The myth: Eggs are packed with cholesterol so should be avoided.

The makeover: Eggs (like shrimp, crab, lobster, cuttlefish, squid, octopus, and liver) are certainly higher in cholesterol than many other foods. As a result, in the past, health experts recommended eating fewer of them to keep blood cholesterol levels in check. However, we now know that it is saturated fat, rather than cholesterol in food that has a greater impact on blood cholesterol levels. That's why health professionals now recommend eating fewer foods that contain saturates, such as fatty meats, whole milk, butter, lard, cream, pastry, cakes, and cookies. Meanwhile, the American Heart Foundation and American College of Nutrition no longer say it's necessary to limit eggs, "as long as one's total cholesterol is limited to no more than 300 milligrams per day."

How much fat is in cream? (per 3½ oz)

Half and half cream	12g
Light cream	20g
Whipping cream	30g
Creme fraiche	40g
Double cream	48g
Clotted cream	55–60g

Myth makeover

The myth: Crème fraîche is healthier than cream.

The makeover: It might sound healthier, but with up to 40 percent fat, it's on a par with whipping cream and contains twice as much fat as sour cream, which it's often used as an alternative to. Lower-fat varieties are available, but still check the label.

Cream

Here's the bad news—all traditional creams are high in fat, so it's best to avoid them completely. Lower-fat, reduced-fat and half-fat varieties are certainly better options if you have to use cream, but this doesn't automatically mean that they are low in fat. Lighter versions of heavy cream, for example, may still contain around 25 percent fat. As explained before, if you want a creamy taste, then yogurt or fromage frais can often be used instead.

Fats and oils

There's no getting away from it, but fats and oils are all high in fat, including reduced-fat spreads. All oils, whether olive, canola, sunflower, or corn oil, are 100 percent fat—it's the type of fat that differs among them. Olive oil and canola oil, for example, have a high proportion of monounsaturated fats, while sunflower and corn oil are richer in polyunsaturated fats. It's certainly better to opt for these oils rather than hard fats, which tend to be much higher in artery-clogging saturated fats. But to follow a low-fat diet, you still need to watch the quantity you use. And if you're not convinced, it's worth remembering that just one tablespoon of any oil contains 11g fat!

Most oils are predominantly rich in heart-healthy polyunsaturated and monounsaturated fats, but the exceptions to this are palm oil, which contains around 45 percent saturates, and coconut oil, which has around 85 percent saturates.

Hard fats are not only high in total fat, but they are also loaded with saturates. Lard, dripping, and ghee (clarified butter), for example, are almost 100 percent fat, but more than half of the fat in dripping, two-thirds of the fat in ghee and 40 percent of the fat in lard, is saturated fat. Butter is 82 percent fat, with two-thirds of this being saturated fat—adding just one teaspoonful to your toast will add 4g fat.

Margarines and spreads can vary considerably in their fat content from brand to brand, ranging from around 55–80 percent fat. The same goes for reduced-fat and "light" spreads. They are certainly a better option for helping to cut down on fat, but it really is worth checking the nutrition information on the packaging, as they can vary dramatically from around 15–40 percent fat.

Finally, it's best to avoid using suet in dishes. Beef suet is around 82 percent fat, and even lower-fat versions of vegetable suet contain around 60 percent fat.

Ways to use less oil

- Always measure oil used for cooking with a teaspoon or tablespoon. Pouring straight from the bottle means you'll end up using more.
- Use nonstick pans—you won't need to use as much oil in cooking.
- Use a spray oil—10 sprays provides around 1g fat. If you don't want to use a branded spray, invest in a spray dispenser and fill it with your favourite brand of oil.
- Always wait until oil is hot before adding ingredients. Food absorbs far more oil if it's only lukewarm.
- Keep ingredients like vegetables and potatoes in larger pieces—the smaller they are, the greater the surface area they have, and so the more oil they will absorb.
- Spray ingredients like meat, fish and chicken with oil, then add to a hot frying pan or griddle—that way you won't end up using more oil than you need.

Starchy foods

Thinking of starchy foods conjures up mostly images of potatoes, pasta, rice, bread, and noodles. And it's fantastic news, since most of these foods are great low-fat options. Better still, our supermarkets are now stocked with more varieties of low-fat starchy foods than ever before. Sweet potatoes, couscous, bulgar wheat, barley, and quinoa help to add variety to our diet so we don't get bored.

But it's important to make sure that we don't undo all the natural low-fat beauty of these products by swamping them with fat. Adding cream, butter, or oil to starchy foods massively increases their fat content, but adds few nutrients. For example, a 5½ oz serving of potatoes mashed with a little skim milk is virtually fat-free, whereas a 5½ oz serving of potatoes fried in oil contains 10g fat. The golden rule: skip the fat and enjoy carbs on their own wherever possible.

Breakfast cereals can also be a good low-fat option, but if they contain nuts and seeds, the fat content will be higher, so check the label. Nutty muesli in particular can easily be around 10 percent fat. Another breakfast option to watch out for is granola. Its healthy image sadly isn't always matched by a healthy fat content—some brands can contain as much as 25 percent fat as the ingredients are coated in oil before they're baked to form clusters. And always serve cereals with lower-fat dairy products such as fat-free yogurt or skim milk.

Bread is another good choice for a low-fat diet providing you don't smother it in butter, margerine or low-fat spread. But again, the addition of nuts and seeds will push up the fat content. Ciabatta and other Mediterranean-style breads can also be higher in fat than normal bread, as they're often made with olive oil, but it's worth checking the label. Pita bread, bagels, and wraps are a good choice—made even better by the fact that most people don't normally spread them with butter or margarine. English muffins and scones also make good lower-fat snacks (as long as they're not spread with lashings of butter). In contrast, bread products such as croissants, brioches, pastries, and muffins are packed with fat, so are best limited.

Finally, the combination of fat and sugar in foods such as cookies, cakes, doughnuts and desserts might make them taste good, but your waistline and heart won't thank you for it. They are all loaded with fat, much of it saturated.

Fat content of bakery foods (per item)

1 toasted English muffin (40g)	Less than 1g fat	1 fruit scone (48g)	5g fat
1 pita bread (55g)	Less than 1g fat	1 panini (85g)	5g fat
1 slice wholewheat or white bread (38g)	Less than 1g fat	1 slice fruit cake (60g)	8g fat
		1 individual fruit pie (54g)	8g fat
1 bagel (85g)	2g fat	1 jelly doughnut (75g)	11g fat
1 slice ciabatta bread (50g)	2g fat	1 croissant (60g)	12g fat
1 wrap (40g)	3g fat	1 blueberry muffin (72g)	14g fat
1 hot cross bun (50g)	3g fat	1 slice cake with buttercream (60g)	18g fat
1 butter brioche (35g)	4g fat		
1 toasted teacake (55g)	5g fat	1 Danish pastry (110g)	19g fat

Fruits and vegetables

Health experts recommend that we eat five servings of fruit and vegetables every day to stay healthy, and it's good advice. They're packed with vitamins, minerals, and antioxidants, provide plenty of fiber to help fill us up, and tend to be low in calories to help us control our weight. But the majority are also low in fat, making them a great choice for a low-fat diet. Of course, there is always the exception, and in the case of fruit and vegetables, it's avocado. This innocuous-looking fruit is actually loaded with fat—just 1 medium avocado pear contains a massive 28g fat, around 40 percent of the GDA. It's mainly heart-healthy monounsaturated fat, but if you're cutting down on total fat, then it's best to limit the amount you eat.

Pulses such as dried peas, beans and lentils are also low in fat, and are a great choice to include in a low-fat diet as they help to fill us up. Using them in place of some of the meat in dishes is a really easy way to lower the overall fat content of meals, and bulk them up, too, so you don't end up with a tiny portion that leaves you feeling like you're on a diet. Red kidney beans tend to be a popular choice, but it's worth experimenting. Most supermarkets now sell a range of canned pulses including chick peas, puy and green lentils, black-eyed peas, and aduki, borlotti, butter, flageolet, haricot and cannellini beans—good news as you don't have the hassle of soaking dried beans, and then cooking them.

Of course, there are still a few things you need to be aware of when selecting vegetables. Beware of vegetables that are preserved in oil. Antipasti are becoming increasingly popular, but sundried tomatoes, eggplant, zucchini, artichokes, peppers, mushrooms, vine leaves, and olives in jars or from the deli counter are often dripping in oil. If you love the Mediterranean style of eating, look for vegetables that come in water, or try making your own antipasti by brushing vegetables with a little olive oil, and then cooking them on a grill pan or roasting them in the oven. Olives in brine are much lower in fat than those in oil, but they're still salty.

Vegetables and pulse-based dips have a healthy image, but hummus can easily contain 30 percent fat and guacamole around 21 percent fat. Even reduced-fat versions can have 10 percent fat or more. Plus, there's the temptation to dip with chips rather than pita or vegetable crudités. Salsa is a better choice, though the jarred varieties usually contain more fat than fresh ones.

Salads also seem like a healthy option, but if they're smothered with mayonnaise or dressing, all that hard work will be undone. Cole slaw and potato salad are among the worst offenders as they're loaded with mayo. Reduced-fat options are usually available, but check the nutrition information as they can vary in fat content considerably.

A word on dressings and mayo

Regular salad dressings and mayonnaise are packed with fat, so it's worth looking for lower-fat alternatives. A tablespoon of mayonnaise contains around 12g fat, with reduced-fat and light versions having around 4g fat, although some brands go even lower than this, with extra light versions that have just 0.5g fat. Tossing salads with dressings can quickly increase the fat content—a tablespoon contains around 7g fat—so always use a spoon to measure them, rather than pouring liberally from the bottle. Many brands now do reduced-fat and even fat-free versions of popular dressings, so it's worth trying these. Otherwise, go with a splash of good-quality balsamic vinegar.

Snacks

It goes without saying that many popular snacks such as cookies, potato chips, savory snacks, chocolate, and other confectionery are loaded with fat, and so should be limited on a low-fat diet. In general, the plainer the cookie, the less fat it contains, so for example, a plain or honey graham cracker contains less than 1g fat, while a chocolate marshmallow bar contains around 4g. Also, remember that people rarely stop at one! One serving of Oreos is generally calculated as three cookies, containing 7g fat. Cereal bars can contain varying amounts of fat, depending on whether they contain nuts or seeds, so check labels carefully. Granola bars sound healthy, but they can be loaded with fat, and also come in large sizes, so can easily make a dent in your daily fat allowance.

Chips and savory snacks make a significant contribution to fat intakes, so follow the golden rules: check the nutrition information, go for the smallest pack size available, and limit the number of times you eat these foods. Buying family-size packs or tubs is never a good idea, as it's easy to keep on eating them.

Fortunately, there's good news for candy lovers. Confectionery such as fruit pastilles, traditional Turkish delight, hard candies, marshmallows, gummy bears, and jelly beans are all fat-free (but they are still loaded with sugar and empty calories, so it's wise not to eat too many). Toffees and chocolate on the other hand aren't great choices—and don't be fooled into thinking that dark chocolate is a better option. Toffee contains around 17 percent fat, while milk, dark and white chocolate all contain around 30 percent fat.

14 smart snack swaps

Swap this	g fat	For this	g fat	Save this amount of fat
1 large packet of potato chips	17g	2 handfuls of homemade fat-free popcorn	4g	13g
2 slices toast with butter	13g	2 slices toast with 2 tbsp low-fat cream cheese and 1 tomato	3g	10g
1 small bar of chocolate (50g)	15g	1 banana	0g	15g
Large Danish pastry	25g	Currant bun	4g	21g
Jelly doughnut	11g	Iced bun	5g	6g
Ice cream bar	3g	Fruit sherbet bar	0g	3g
Handful of chocolate-coated peanuts	18g	Handful of chocolate-coated raisins	7g	11g
2 chocolate chip cookies	8g	2 plain or honey graham crackers	0.3g	7.7g
Slice of layer cake with buttercream filling	18g	Slice of Battenberg cake	4g	14g
Handful of salted peanuts	16g	Handful of Japanese rice crackers	1g	9g
Large chunk of Cheddar with 4 cream crackers	20g	2 tbsp low-fat cream cheese on 4 rye crackers	3g	17g
5 tbsp garlic dip with a handful of tortilla chips	31g	5 tbsp salsa dip with carrot sticks	0g	31g
3 scoops vanilla ice cream	18g	3 scoops lemon sorbet	1g	17g
5 Belgian chocolates	21g	5 marshmallows	0g	21g

Nuts and seeds

Sadly all nuts and seeds are high in fat, with the exception of chestnuts, which are actually low in fat. Yes, it's mainly heart-healthy fat but that's still no good for a low-fat diet. The golden rules are to control portion sizes—easier said than done if you're a nut lover! Going for fresh nuts in their shells helps as it takes longer to get into them, slowing down the speed you nibble. You can also "dilute" some of the fat by mixing nuts with dried fruit.

Go nuts

Fat content per 3½ oz

Chestnuts	3g	Roasted and salted peanuts	53g	Hazelnuts	64g
Fruit and nut mix	25g	Peanut butter	54g	Brazil nuts	68g
Flax seeds	34g	Mixed nuts	54g	Walnuts	69g
Pumpkin seeds	46g	Pistachio nuts	54g	Pine nuts	69g
Sunflower seeds	48g	Almonds	56g	Pecan nuts	70g
Cashew nuts	49g	Sesame seeds	58g	Macadamia nuts	76g

While nuts are considered high in fats, many people don't know they are also cardioprotective. This is because of the range of nutrients they provide, including heart-healthy monounsaturated fatty acids, naturally occurring plant sterols, fiber, vitamin E, magnesium, potassium, and other naturally occuring plant compounds. So while it's important to avoid an excessive intake of nuts, they can still be incorporated into recipes and used for snacks as part of a low-fat approach to eating.

Drinks

Surprisingly, it's possible to drink loads of fat! And no, we're not talking about chugging down olive oil! Many fluids are actually loaded with fat, so it's wise to think before you drink. Good fat-free choices include water, of course, and also skim milk, pure fruit juices, smoothies, and fruit drinks (although do beware that the latter may contain a lot of added sugar). If you can't bear the thought of skim milk as a drink, go for 1% or reduced fat rather than whole milk—or mix it with fruit to make a shake. Yogurt-based and probiotic drinks can also be a good choice.

With bottles of ready-made milk shakes and drinks, it's always worth checking the label to see how much fat they contain. And avoid shakes from fast-food outlets—a large, healthy-sounding banana or strawberry milk shake can easily contain 14g fat, while a chocolate shake has 15g fat.

Hot drinks aren't usually on the radar when we think about fat, and providing we use low-fat milk in tea or coffee then we really don't need to worry. But if you regularly buy from coffee shops, you may need to think again. A tall cappuccino made with whole milk contains more than 5g fat, while a tall caffé latte has almost 10g. The key is to go "skinny.'" Meanwhile, a hot chocolate with whipped cream can total 26g fat. If you love a chocolate fix, then a mug of homemade hot chocolate made with skim milk is virtually fat-free.

Fortunately, most alcoholic drinks such as beer, cider, wine, sherry, and spirits are fat-free (although they're still packed with calories—alcohol contains almost as many calories per gram as fat). However, cream liqueurs are the ones to avoid, as are cocktails made with cream, or coconut milk.

Making low-fat food taste great

Fat helps to add flavor and moisture to food, so most chefs agree that if you're going to dramatically reduce the fat content of meals, then you need to work harder to make food taste great. The good news is that it's very easy to do.

Marinating lean meat, skinless chicken, and fish is a great way to add flavor, keep it tender, and help prevent it from drying out during cooking. The key is to go for low-fat marinades. In particular, acidic ingredients such as lemon juice, vinegar, wine, and yogurt help break down the proteins in meat, tenderizing them. But if you're using a marinade that includes an acidic ingredient, you'll need to use a glass or ceramic container to stop the food from discoloring. Depending on the size of the meat portion, you can marinate for anything from 20 minutes to several hours, although yogurt marinades are best after 8 hours or overnight.

Rubs and seasoning powders are also a great way to add flavor, although some can be really high in salt, so steer clear of additional seasoning if you use them. Most supermarkets now stock a wide selection, so start experimenting.

Poaching is a great cooking method for keeping meat and fish moist. Salmon is classically poached in a court-bouillon (a light stock that's usually based on an acidic ingredient such as white wine, vinegar or lemon juice combined with spices). Another flavorsome poaching liquor that goes particularly well with white fish, is a mixture of white wine and stock flavored with lemon, and a bouquet garni. But you can also use skim milk for poaching fish and then use the liquor to make a low-fat béchamel sauce. Chicken can also be poached to add variety to your diet. And even red meat such as beef can be poached in red wine, mixed with beef stock and herbs.

Meanwhile, it's a good idea to keep your kitchen stocked with a variety of low-fat natural flavor enhancers. Good choices to keep handy include wine, garlic, citrus juices, pepper, fresh and dried herbs, spices, reduced-salt soy sauce, fish sauce, tomato paste, Worcestershire sauce, and a selection of stock options.

Easy tips for cutting fat

- Always eat breakfast—it's the easiest meal of the day to make low fat, but do steer clear of fatty baked products such as croissants, Danish pastries, and doughnuts.
- Monitor your portion sizes—the bigger the portion, the more fat it will contain, so downsize your servings, and fill any gaps with vegetables or salad.
- Swap a couple of meat dishes for veggie dishes each week—you don't need to be a vegetarian to enjoy meat-free meals.
- Include a couple of portions of fish each week—white fish and shellfish are particularly good low-fat choices.
- Broil, grill, dry roast, bake, poach, or steam food, rather than frying or roasting it.
- Trim any visible fat off meat, and remove the skin from chicken before you cook it.
- When you're shopping, compare labels and pick products with less fat.
- Choose lower-fat dairy products.
- Put more vegetables and pulses and less meat in casseroles, stews, and curries.
- Make meat dishes such as casseroles, Bolognese sauce, stews, and curries a day in advance and store in the refrigerator. Any fat should harden, making it easier for you to remove it before reheating.
- Don't use roasting juices to make gravy without skimming the fat off first.
- Measure oil for cooking with a tablespoon, rather than pouring it straight from the bottle.
- If you do choose something high in fat to eat, pick something low in fat to go with it—for example, a baked potato instead of fries.
- If you're using a moist filling in sandwiches, skip the butter or spread.
- When you do use spread, go for a reduced-fat variety, and choose one that is soft straight from the refrigerator so it's easier to spread thinly.

Breakfasts

All-in-one scrambled eggs and bacon

Per serving

278 cals   6.2g fiber
7.2g fat   1.7g salt
2g saturated fat
3.3g sugar   **3g fat per 100g**

Scrambled eggs are always popular, but the days of adding butter and cream will have to remain a distant memory. Here, I've decreased the fat by reducing the yolk content, and increasing the quantity of egg whites.

Serves 4

2 slices Canadian bacon, fat removed, cut into strips
2 scallions, finely sliced
8 cherry tomatoes, halved
spray of olive oil
14 oz canned cannellini beans, drained and rinsed
2 whole free-range eggs + 5 egg whites, lightly beaten together
1 teaspoon horseradish
2 teaspoons snipped chives
4 thick slices of whole wheat toast

Cook the bacon, scallions, and tomatoes over medium heat in a nonstick frying pan with a light spray of oil until lightly softened, about 6–8 minutes. Add the beans, and fry for 2 minutes.

Meanwhile, combine the eggs with the horseradish and chives. Season to taste.

Pour the eggs over the bacon, and stir to combine, constantly dragging up the edges of the eggs to the center, producing curds. Once cooked to your liking—I prefer my eggs quite soft—spoon onto the four slices of toast.

Tip

Remember that even after you've turned off the heat, the eggs will continue to cook, so work at a brisk pace in the latter stages.

An alternative bacon sandwich

Per serving

193 cals   3.7g fiber

4.1g fat   2.1g salt

1.2g saturated fat

6.8g sugar   **1.3g fat per 100g**

One of my favorite breakfasts, prior to the low-fat era, was crisp bacon with herbed tomatoes, and toasted rye bread. Here, I've substituted thinly shaved sandwich ham, which helps control the saturated fat count.

Serves 4

8 vine-ripened tomatoes, halved horizontally

spray of olive oil

1 teaspoon soft thyme leaves

3 garlic cloves, peeled

¼ teaspoon sea salt

1¼ cups (7 oz) sliced button mushrooms

1 tablespoon balsamic vinegar

8 basil leaves, torn

2 tablespoons chopped parsley

6 oz shaved ham slices

4 slices of your favorite seeded bread, toasted

Preheat the oven to 375°F.

Place the tomatoes, cut-side up, in a shallow baking pan, and season with black pepper. Spray with a light mist of oil.

Chop together the thyme, garlic, and sea salt until you have a herby paste. In the final stages, this is best achieved by using the back of the knife to crush the mix until very smooth. Spread a little on each of the tomato halves, then place in the oven, and cook for 25–30 minutes, checking from time to time. You're looking for the tomatoes to be really soft without collapsing.

Lightly oil a frying pan and cook the mushrooms over high heat for 5–8 minutes, stirring regularly. Add the balsamic vinegar, then fold in the basil and parsley, and allow to wilt in the heat of the mushrooms. Season well.

Heat the ham (or not) gently, and serve with the toast, mushrooms, and tomatoes. Warn your diners that the tomatoes will be very hot.

Per serving

216 cals   3.1g fiber

4.1g fat   3.5g salt

1g saturated fat

6.3g sugar   **1.5g fat per 100g**

Breakfast on rye

Breakfast—so often a neglected meal of the day, and it's so important. It's just a case of having a few of the right ingredients handy: plan your ingredients, and the rest is child's play.

Serves 1

1 slice of rye bread

1 teaspoon Dijon mustard

3 tablespoons low-fat cottage cheese

1 slice smoked salmon

1 tomato, thinly sliced

8 slices of cucumber

1 scallion, thinly sliced

1 teaspoon lemon juice

Toast the rye bread, then spread with the mustard, and smooth over the cottage cheese. Next, layer with the smoked salmon, plus a grind of black pepper, followed by the tomato and cucumber slices, slightly overlapping. Scatter with the scallion, and drizzle with lemon juice.

Tip

Rye toasts well from frozen, and it's great for those on a gluten-free diet.

Moms on the run

Per serving

306 cals | 3.4g fiber
1g fat | 0.6g salt
0.2g saturated fat |
46g sugar | **0.4g fat per 100g**

Breakfast is definitely an important meal, but cereal can get a little dull, so here's a summery alternative.

Makes 1

1 slice of rye bread, or other bread
2 tablespoons fat-free Greek yogurt
1 banana, cut into chunks
4 strawberries, quartered
¼ teaspoon ground cinnamon
3 teaspoons honey

Toast the rye bread. Combine the remaining ingredients and dollop on top of the toast…simple.

A gutsy egg-white breakfast

Per serving

122 cals | 2.7g fiber
1.3g fat | 1g salt
0.4g saturated fat |
6.8g sugar | **0.4g fat per 100g**

When I was in America, I noticed a trend for egg-white omelets and, I'll be honest, I thought they must be mad—an omelet with no yolk, therefore no flavor. They were, of course, paranoid about cholesterol in an egg yolk. But we now know that, for many of us, our bodies deal very effectively with dietary cholesterol, and that eggs are not only safe to eat, but also one of the original all-around superfoods. There is, however, fat in the egg yolk, so low-fat food should include them sparingly. Here I've developed an egg-white omelet with guts and flavor.

Serves 4

12 free-range egg whites
1 onion, finely chopped
spray of olive oil
⅔ cup (4 oz) green peas, defrosted
2 handfuls of baby spinach leaves, washed
2 tablespoons snipped chives
1 tablespoon chopped parsley
2 tomatoes, seeded and diced
12 basil leaves, torn
½ cup (4 oz) low-fat cottage cheese
3 tablespoons fat-free Greek yogurt

Whisk the egg whites in a very clean bowl to soft peaks.

Meanwhile, spray the onion with olive oil, and cook in a large frying pan over medium heat until soft, but without color, about 8 minutes. Add the green peas, spinach, chives, and parsley, and cook for 2 minutes, stirring constantly, until the spinach has wilted. Fold in the tomato and basil, then set aside to cool.

Remove a quarter of the whisked egg white to a bowl, whisk again, then fold in one quarter of the herb and tomato mixture.

Lightly spray a nonstick omelet pan with oil, spoon in the combined egg and herb mixture, then spread evenly, and allow to cook over medium heat until the omelet is golden brown on the bottom. Sprinkle over one quarter of the cottage cheese and yogurt, season with salt and pepper, then fold the omelet to enclose the cheese. Slide onto a warm plate, and keep warm while you cook the other three omelets.

Tip

Some supermarkets now stock pasteurized egg whites in cartons.

Banana bircher muesli

Per serving

227 cals   2.9g fiber

1.7g fat   0.1g salt

0.1g saturated fat

38.2g sugar   **0.7g fat per 100g**

Bircher muesli is a recipe in which oats are soaked overnight. The contrast of the hot and cold makes this breakfast perfect for a cold morning. When you cook bananas in their skins, you get this wonderful fluffy souffléed effect.

Serves 4

⅔ cup (2 oz) toasted rolled oats

¾ cup (6 fl oz) apple juice

4 bananas

1 tablespoon honey

2 apples, cored and diced

4 tablespoons fat-free Greek yogurt

Soak the oats overnight in the apple juice.

The next day, preheat the oven to 350°F.

Place the bananas on a rack in the oven and cook for 20–30 minutes, until blackened and very soft when gently squeezed.

Combine the soaked muesli with the honey, apple, and yogurt, and spoon a quarter into each breakfast bowl.

Using the tip of a sharp knife, cut down the natural seam of the banana skin, and peel back a section of skin. Scoop out the banana flesh with a teaspoon and place on top of the yogurt mixture. Eat while the banana is still hot.

Multi-fiber, multigrain, multi-fruit oatmeal

Per serving

286 cals   2.5g fiber

3.7 fat   0.4g salt

0.5 saturated fat

23.5g sugar   **1g fat per 100g**

Oatmeal is the perfect way to start your day. This slow-release, fiber-rich food keeps you feeling full until lunchtime, but oatmeal on its own can be a bit repetitive, however, the addition of other grains and dried fruit adds a little more texture, and lots more flavor.

dry oatmeal mixture
(makes 20 servings)

4½ cups (14 oz) rolled oats

1 cup (4 oz) rice flakes

1 cup (4 oz) barley flakes

1 cup (4 oz) rye flakes

¾ cup (6 oz) millet

1 tablespoon sesame seeds

1 tablespoon flaxseed

1 tablespoon sunflower seeds

½ cup (3 oz) golden raisins

⅔ cup (4 oz) dried apricots, chopped

⅓ cup (2 oz) dried cherries

scant ½ cup (2 oz) dried cranberries

¼ cup (1 oz) goji berries

Mix all the dry ingredients in a large bowl, making sure that everything is evenly distributed. This mixture can be stored in an airtight container, to be used as required.

To cook the oatmeal for four people, weigh out 8 oz of the mixture into a saucepan, add a pinch of salt, then add 9 fl oz water and 8 fl oz skim milk. Stir well, then leave to rest for 15 minutes, which helps all the grains to absorb the liquid. Stir well, then add another 9 fl oz water and 8 fl oz milk.

Bring to a boil over medium heat, stirring regularly, then reduce the heat and simmer for 12–15 minutes until the mixture is smooth, thick, and creamy. Serve with extra milk, a tablespoon of fat-free Greek yogurt, and a teaspoon of soft light brown sugar.

Fruity quinoa

Per serving (based on 6 servings)

331 cals	6.4g fiber
6.8g fat	0.2g salt
0.6g saturated fat	
45.4g sugar	**2.8g fat per 100g**

Quinoa (pronounced "keen-wa") has been featuring quite a lot in my diet recently as I've been trying to avoid gluten. It has an interesting, slightly nutty taste, with a little chew on the palate. I love it, so give it a shot.

Serves 4–6

1½ cups (6 oz) quinoa, rinsed well
    and drained
2 scant cups (15 fl oz) unsweetened
    orange juice
²⁄₃ cup (3½ oz) dried figs, chopped
²⁄₃ cup (4 oz) dried apple, chopped
²⁄₃ cup (4 oz) dried apricots, chopped
¼ cup (1½ oz) candied citrus peel
¼ cup (1 oz) chopped hazelnuts
¼ cup (1 oz) sunflower seeds
grated zest of 1 orange
1 apple, grated
1¹⁄₃ cups (5¼ oz) raspberries
2 teaspoons chopped mint

Put the quinoa and orange juice in a saucepan. Bring to a boil, then reduce the heat and simmer gently for 10 minutes, by which time the liquid should have been absorbed. Cover and leave to cool for 15 minutes.

Transfer the quinoa to a bowl, and combine with the dried fruits, nuts, seeds, orange zest, and grated apple.

Spoon the mixture into six bowls, and top with the raspberries and a dollop of fat-free Greek yogurt. Time to eat…

Tip

The cooked quinoa will last 3–4 days in the refrigerator. Reheat in a microwave, then combine with the fruits.

Per serving (based on 6 servings)

11 cals	0.5g fiber
0.1g fat	0g salt
0g saturated fat	
1.9g sugar	**0g fat per 100g**

Cucumber mint fizz

This is beautifully refreshing; a drink you can enjoy throughout the summer, without getting bored. As a bonus, it is pretty calorie-free.

Serves 4–6

1 cucumber
12 mint leaves
1 teaspoon superfine sugar
juice of 2 limes
6½ cups (1½ quarts) carbonated water

Using a potato peeler, peel the cucumber into long ribbons continuously until you reach the seeds, then turn the cucumber around and repeat until all you are left with are the seeds (which you will discard).

Place the mint in a mortar or bowl, and pound or muddle the mint with the sugar until you have a rough paste. Spoon into a large pitcher with the cucumber ribbons and the lime juice. This mixture can be made ahead and refrigerated until ready to drink.

Pour on the carbonated water and stir to combine. Pour into ice-filled glasses.

Cosmopolitan breakfast blast

Per serving

162 cals

1.1g fat

0g saturated fat

17.2g sugar

4g fiber

0g salt

0.4g fat per 100g

There have been many creations on the cocktail front using cranberry juice, but the flavor also suits breakfast fruits really well. An easy way of getting some of your five a day, this concoction can be prepared the night before as most of us are in a rush first thing in the morning.

Serves 4

1 red or pink grapefruit

1 yellow grapefruit

3 navel oranges

1 kiwi fruit

12 mint leaves, shredded

1¼ cups (10 fl oz) cranberry juice

4 tablespoons toasted rolled oats

Carefully cut all the skin and pith away from the citrus fruits, and pare the skin from the kiwi fruit.

Working over a bowl to catch the juices, carefully cut the citrus fruit between the membranes to obtain segments. Squeeze any remaining juice from the core into the bowl with the fruit. Cut the kiwi in half vertically, then cut each half in half again, creating four segments, and combine with the other fruits. Fold in the mint, and pour in the cranberry juice.

Divide the mixture between four glasses, making sure that each gets one segment of kiwi. Scatter a tablespoon of toasted oats over each serving.

Tip

Feel free to use muesli instead of toasted oats, but beware of the nut content of some mueslis.

Per serving (based on 3 servings)

145 cals

0.8g fat

0.2g saturated fat

33g sugar

7.9g fiber

0.2g salt

0.2g fat per 100g

My favorite morning pick-me-up

With my own juicer on the market, I've had hours of fun developing different juices: some great, some pretty grim! (I can't get my head around wheatgrass—the "no pain, no gain" school of thought is not for me.) I keep coming back to this combination, which is a very pleasant drink, and undoubtedly does you a great deal of good.

Serves 2–3

2 raw beets, washed but not peeled

6 carrots, peeled if not organic

4 dessert apples

1 stick of celery

1-inch slice of fresh ginger

ice cubes

Put all the ingredients through your centrifugal juicer (juice extractor) on the hard fruit or fast setting. Stir to combine, then pour over ice cubes.

Tip

Beet juice should never be drunk on its own as the body is a bit overwhelmed by its nutrients. Beets are also very hard, so don't push too hard on the plunger.

Black currant breakfast smoothie

Per serving

262 cals

2.9g fat

0.1g saturated fat

27.4g sugar

4.3g fiber

0.1g salt

0.8g fat per 100g

Who needs Ribena when you can get masses of vitamin C from fresh black currants? And the oats pack in some good fiber—a slow-release breakfast in a glass.

Serves 4

2 bananas, roughly cut

1 cup (7 oz) black currants, stripped from their stems

1 cup (4 oz) rolled oats

2 tablespoons honey

1 cup (8 oz) fat-free Greek yogurt

1¼ cups (10 fl oz) skim milk

12 ice cubes

Process all the ingredients in your blender and serve in four glasses.

Tip

As long as you use the core ingredients above, you can use any ripe fruits, such as blackberries, strawberries, raspberries, peaches, apricots, and nectarines.

Exotic fruit crush

Per serving

222 cals

1.3g fat

0.2g saturated fat

48.3g sugar

5.7g fiber

0g salt

0.4g fat per 100g

This is a lovely breakfast drink, especially good for those who are lactose intolerant. It's very healthy, giving you a fabulous dose of antioxidants.

Serves 4

8 dried apricots, soaked in boiling water for 15 minutes, then roughly chopped

6 slices dried apple, soaked in boiling water for 10 minutes, then roughly chopped

⅔ cup raspberries

2 bananas, roughly chopped

1 mango, peeled, pitted, and roughly chopped

2 tablespoons wheat germ

2½ cups (20 fl oz) unsweetened apple juice

1 teaspoon roughly chopped mint leaves

10 ice cubes

Place all the ingredients in a blender and process until thick and smooth. Pour into four chilled glasses and serve immediately.

Tip

This is a great way to use up what's left in the fruit bowl, and at the same time get a valuable dose of healthy ingredients. Play around with different fruit combinations.

Fruit and fiber yogurt layer

Per serving

307 cals   4.7g fiber

2.9g fat   0.4g salt

0.4g saturated fat

42.6g sugar   **1.2g fat per 100g**

This looks beautiful, which means that your eyes will be telling your brain to enjoy it. It's easy to make, colorful, tasty, and a great start to your day.

Serves 4

8 strawberries, hulled and sliced, plus 2 for garnish

1¼ cups (5 oz) muesli

1²⁄₃ cups (13 oz) fat-free Greek yogurt

2 kiwi fruit, peeled and sliced

1 mango, peeled, pitted, and diced

3 tablespoons dried cranberries

3 tablespoons dried cherries

2 tablespoons dark brown sugar

Divide the strawberry slices between four glasses, and top with a little muesli and a dollop of yogurt. Repeat the layers, using different fruits each time, finishing with a layer of yogurt. Top with a little brown sugar, and some strawberry slices.

Tip

This can be prepared the night before and refrigerated. The brown sugar will melt, creating a delicious puddle of sweetness.

Mediterranean vegetable tortilla

Per serving

203 cals   1.6g fiber

8.3g fat   1.6g salt

2.4g saturated fat

7.2g sugar   **2.3g fat per 100g**

This solid, packed omelet is not only good for breakfast, but it works well served at room temperature for lunch or supper, and it is also an excellent picnic food.

Serves 4

spray of olive oil

2 slices Canadian bacon, cut into strips

4 scallions, halved lengthwise

4 asparagus spears, halved lengthwise

4 artichoke hearts (in water, from a jar), drained on paper towels and halved

4 roasted red peppers (not in oil), drained on paper towels and halved lengthwise

12 basil leaves, torn

4 free-range eggs

4 egg whites

1 cup (8 oz) fat-free Greek yogurt

Preheat the oven to 325°F.

Spray a light coating of oil onto the base and sides of a 7½-inch square cake pan. Line the base and sides with baking parchment paper.

Spray a light coating of oil onto a nonstick frying pan, and cook the bacon over medium heat for 6–8 minutes, then add the scallions and asparagus, and cook for 4–5 minutes more, until lightly softened. Combine with the artichokes and red peppers.

Spoon the mixture into the cake pan, making sure that each "quarter" has a little of each vegetable, then season, and sprinkle with basil.

Whisk the eggs, egg whites, and yogurt until well-combined, then pour over the vegetables. Prod with a fork to ensure that the egg mixture filters down between the vegetables.

Bake in the oven for 35 minutes, or until set. Allow to cool slightly before cutting into four squares.

Low-fat ricotta cakes with roast tomato

Per serving

127 cals   1.8g fiber

6.1g fat   0.4g salt

2.9g saturated fat

6.9g sugar   **2.9g fat per 100g**

This is a perfect weekend breakfast, requiring very little preparation and a slow cooking time. It also offers something a little bit different.

Serves 4

spray of olive oil

½ onion, finely chopped

1 garlic clove, finely chopped

2 teaspoons candied citrus peel, roughly chopped

½ cup (3 oz) frozen leaf spinach, defrosted, or 11 oz fresh baby spinach, washed, cooked and squeezed

½ cup (4 oz) ricotta cheese

½ cup (4 oz) low-fat cottage cheese

1 free-range egg, lightly beaten

2 teaspoons chopped dill

¼ teaspoon grated nutmeg

4 stalks cherry tomatoes on the vine (about six on each)

1 tablespoon sherry or balsamic vinegar

Preheat the oven to 400°F. Spray four holes of a muffin tin with oil.

Spray a frying pan with a light coating of oil, then, over medium heat, cook the onion and garlic for 8–10 minutes until soft, but not colored. Add the candied peel and spinach, and cook until any liquid has evaporated, stirring continuously. Allow to cool.

Add the spinach mixture to the two cheeses in a bowl, then stir in the egg and dill. Season to taste. Divide the mixture between the four muffin holes, and bake in the oven for 15–20 minutes, until golden.

Meanwhile, place the tomatoes on a baking sheet, spray with oil, season with salt and pepper, and cook in the same oven for 12–15 minutes.

Drizzle the sherry or balsamic vinegar over the tomatoes, and serve on warm plates with the ricotta cakes.

Soups and snacks

Per serving (based on 6 servings)

236 cals	5g fiber
5.7g fat	0.6g salt
1.5g saturated fat	
8.9g sugar	**0.8g fat per 100g**

A take on minestrone

This soup has got it all: carbs, protein, loads of goodness, and lots of flavor. For even lower fat, you can omit the pancetta, but it does give the soup a great flavor. See "A different green salad" on page 214 for some info on the edamame beans.

Serves 4–6

1 teaspoon olive oil

4 slices pancetta, trimmed and finely diced

1 onion, finely chopped

1 leek, washed and finely sliced

3 garlic cloves, finely chopped

1 stick of celery, finely sliced

1 carrot, peeled and finely diced

4 new potatoes, washed, skin on, cut into ½-inch dice

1 tablespoon tomato paste

2 sprigs of thyme

2 bay leaves

2 quarts fresh chicken or vegetable stock, preferably homemade

14 oz canned chopped tomatoes

1 cup (4 oz) macaroni

½ cup (3 oz) frozen podded edamame beans

14 oz canned green kidney (flageolet) beans, drained and rinsed

½ cup (5 oz) cauliflower florets

1 large zucchini, cut into ½-inch dice

⅔ cup (4 oz) frozen green peas, defrosted

12 basil leaves

Heat the oil in a large saucepan, add the pancetta, and fry for 3 minutes, then drain off all but one teaspoonful of fat. Add the onion, and cook over medium heat for 8 minutes, until starting to soften, stirring from time to time.

Add the leeks, garlic, celery, carrot, and new potatoes, stir to combine, then add the tomato paste, thyme, and bay leaves, and stir again.

Add the stock and tomatoes, and bring to a boil, reduce the heat, and simmer for 20 minutes. Add the macaroni, and cook for 10 minutes, then add the edamame beans, and cook for 2 minutes before adding the kidney beans, cauliflower, zucchini, and green peas. Cook for 4 minutes, then season.

Finally, sprinkle over the basil and serve.

Tip

Obviously, you can vary the vegetables to suit your taste. Just make sure you add root vegetables at the beginning of cooking, and any vegetables that grow above ground toward the end.

A gutsy chicken and corn soup

Per serving	
296 cals	6.2g fiber
2.1g fat	1g salt
0.4 saturated fat	
13.2g sugar	**0.3g fat per 100g**

I can't put my finger on why, but there's something magical about the marriage of corn and chicken. This combo has been with us for some time, whether in Chinese cooking or in American chowders—simple, filling, and delicious.

Serves 4

6 oz boneless, skinless
   chicken breasts
1¼ quarts good chicken stock,
   preferably homemade
1 onion, finely diced
1 carrot, peeled and finely diced
1 stick of celery, finely diced
3 medium russet potatoes, peeled
   and cut into ½-inch cubes
½ red bell pepper, seeded
   and finely diced
2 bay leaves
¼ teaspoon grated nutmeg
¼ teaspoon sweet paprika
¼ teaspoon ground white pepper
kernels from 1 cooked corn on the cob
14 oz canned creamed corn
2 teaspoons low-sodium soy sauce
¾ cup (6 fl oz) skim milk
2 teaspoons chopped dill
2 teaspoons chopped parsley

Place the chicken breast in a saucepan with the stock, bring slowly to a boil, reduce the heat and simmer for 8 minutes. Take out the chicken, place on a plate and cover loosely with plastic wrap to prevent it from drying out while it cools. When cool enough to handle, either pull the chicken into shreds using 2 forks, or cut into small dice; set aside.

Meanwhile add the onion, carrot, celery, potatoes, bell pepper, bay leaves, nutmeg, paprika, and white pepper to the stock. Bring to a boil, reduce the heat, and simmer for 15 minutes until the potatoes are cooked.

Stir in the corn kernels, creamed corn, soy sauce, and the skim milk, and cook for 3 minutes, stirring without boiling. Finally fold in the chicken and herbs, check the seasoning, and serve very hot with bread.

Smoked haddock and potato soup

Per serving
137 cals   0.7g fiber
1.2g fat   1.5g salt
0.2g saturated fat
8g sugar   **0.3g fat per 100g**

A little bit of Scotland meets India in this slightly bizarre, but enjoyable winter soup.

Serves 6

1 onion, roughly chopped
1 stick of celery, roughly chopped
1 carrot, peeled and roughly chopped
2 cloves
2 bay leaves
1 tablespoon curry paste
1 scant quart (30 fl oz) water
12 oz smoked haddock (finnan haddie)
scant 2 cups (15 fl oz) skim milk
2 tablespoons mango chutney, diced
1¼ cups (12 oz) hot mashed potato
juice of 1 lemon
½ cup (4 oz) low-fat fromage frais
3 tablespoons chopped parsley

Put the onion, celery, carrot, cloves, bay leaves, and curry paste in a saucepan with the water and bring to a boil. Reduce the heat, and simmer for 15 minutes.

Add the smoked haddock to the pan and cook for 5 minutes. Scoop out the fish, and when it's cool enough to handle, remove any skin and bone, and return these (but not the flesh) to the poaching liquid. This should cook for another 10 minutes before being strained, with the solids discarded. Return the liquid to the saucepan, and put it back on the heat.

Flake the fish and return it to the stock with the milk and chutney. Bring to a boil, then whisk in the mashed potato to emulsify with the fish and liquid.

Fold in the lemon juice and fromage frais with the chopped parsley. Reheat, but *do not boil*. Check the seasoning, then serve piping hot.

Chicken, asparagus, and noodle soup

Per serving
175 cals   2.2g fiber
1.1g fat   0.1g salt
0.2g saturated fat
2.3g sugar   **0.2g fat per 100g**

This soup requires a decent homemade stock, if possible, although some of the proprietary brands would do at a pinch (but watch out for the salt levels). This is a light, refreshing meal in a bowl.

Serves 4

1 quart good fresh chicken stock,
    preferably homemade
1 skinless chicken breast, very thinly sliced
3 scallions, finely sliced
½ cup (3 oz) frozen green peas, defrosted
2 teaspoons chopped tarragon
8 oz fresh asparagus, 1-inch tips cut,
    and the remainder thinly sliced
¾ cup (6 fl oz) dry white wine
½ teaspoon crushed garlic
3 oz thin vermicelli (rice noodles)
handful of baby spinach

Heat the stock in a large saucepan, then add the chicken breast, and cook for 1 minute.

Add the scallions, peas, tarragon, asparagus tips and slices, white wine, and garlic, bring back to a boil, then cook for 3 minutes.

Add the vermicelli and spinach, and cook for 2 minutes until the noodles have softened, and the spinach has wilted. Check the seasoning and serve piping hot.

Tip

You could use leftover cooked chicken, instead of raw, if you like.

Crab and cilantro soup

Per serving
166 cals   1.5g fiber
9.9g fat   3.7g salt
5.2g saturated fat
5.1g sugar   **1g fat per 100g**

There's a real earthy blast of heat from the Thai red curry paste in this soup. There's no need to spend fortunes on really good hand-picked white crabmeat, although it would be nice; you'll often find brown and white crabmeat sold separately.

Serves 6

2 teaspoons vegetable or canola oil

1 onion, finely diced

2 tablespoons Thai red curry paste

1 red bell pepper, seeded and
    finely diced

2 garlic cloves, crushed to a paste with
    a little sea salt

1 stalk of lemongrass, left whole, but
    bruised all over with the back of a knife

2 kaffir lime leaves, left whole

1¼ cups (10 fl oz) light coconut milk

30 fl oz dashi or fish stock

1 cup (6 oz) brown crabmeat

1 tablespoon anchovy sauce

½ cup (3 oz) frozen green peas,
    defrosted

¾ cup (4 oz) fresh or drained canned
    lump white crabmeat

1 tablespoon nam pla (fish sauce)

1 tablespoon fresh lime juice

4 tablespoons chopped cilantro

2 red peppers, seeded and finely sliced

3 scallions, finely sliced

Heat the oil in a large wok or saucepan, then cook the onion for 6 minutes, until starting to soften. Add the curry paste, stir to combine, and cook for 1 minute before adding the bell pepper, garlic, lemongrass, and lime leaves. Stir, then cook for 3 minutes.

Add the coconut milk, stock, brown crabmeat, and anchovy sauce. Bring to a boil, stirring from time to time, and cook for 10 minutes.

Add the peas and white crabmeat, and cook for 3 minutes, then add the fish sauce and lime juice. Remove the lemongrass and discard.

Top the soup with the cilantro, chiles, and scallions.

Cauliflower and arugula soup

Per serving (based on 8 servings)
118 cals
3.3g fat
0.8g saturated fat
8.6g sugar
3.2g fiber
1.9g salt
0.6g fat per 100g

Cauliflower makes a delicious soup, and with the addition of arugula, you get a lovely peppery aftertaste. I've added crunch by including some fast-roasted cauliflower florets.

Serves 6–8

1 tablespoon vegetable oil
1 onion, roughly chopped
2 garlic cloves, roughly chopped
1 stick of celery, thinly sliced
1 carrot, peeled and thinly sliced
1 large floury potato, peeled and
   thinly sliced
1 large cauliflower (2¼ lb), two-thirds
   roughly chopped (including
   the core), one-third cut into
   small florets
1 bay leaf
½ teaspoon chopped thyme leaves
1 quart good vegetable stock
1 pint skim milk
1 teaspoon ground cumin
2 handfuls of arugula leaves
½ teaspoon ground white pepper

Preheat the oven to 425°F.

Heat half the vegetable oil in a large saucepan. Add the onion, garlic, celery, and carrot and cook for 8–10 minutes over medium to low heat to lightly color and soften the onion. Add the potato, and cook until the potato starts to stick, and the edges start to soften.

Add the roughly chopped cauliflower, bay leaf, thyme, and stock to the pan. Bring to a boil, then reduce the heat and simmer for 15–20 minutes. Add the milk, and warm through without letting the soup boil.

Meanwhile, toss the cauliflower florets with the remaining oil in a bowl, then add the cumin and toss again. Place on a baking sheet and roast for 12–15 minutes, until the cauliflower begins to brown, but still retains some bite.

Process the soup in a blender with the arugula and white pepper. Blend it in batches, then pass through a fine sieve. Check the seasoning.

Drain the roast cauliflower and divide between the hot soup bowls. Pour in the soup and serve immediately.

Hot and sour shrimp soup

Per serving
126 cals   1.4g fiber
2.3g fat   5.2g salt
0.6g saturated fat
11.1g sugar   **0.5g fat per 100g**

Loosely based on that Thai favorite Tom Yum Goong, this soup is something I often knock up for a very light, very healthy lunch. It's a great alternative to creamy soups, but still tastes amazing. You can vary the fish if you want. It's equally as good with flakes or chunks of white fish, scallops, or oysters. Vary the heat by adding more or less chiles.

Serves 4

1 quart dashi or vegetable stock

1 onion, peeled and grated

3 tablespoons galangal or fresh ginger, peeled and julienned

1 lemongrass stalk, outside leaves removed, and bruised with the back of a knife

3 kaffir lime leaves, finely shredded

3 garlic cloves, crushed to a paste with a little sea salt

2 bird's eye red peppers, finely sliced, then bruised

3 oz fresh shiitake mushrooms, stalks discarded and caps quartered

12 cherry tomatoes, halved horizontally

12 peeled raw tiger shrimp, deveined

small handful of baby spinach leaves

4 tablespoons brown rice miso

juice of 2 limes

2 tablespoons chopped cilantro leaves

1 tablespoon honey

½ cup (4 fl oz) clear apple juice

Heat the stock in a non-reactive saucepan with the onion, galangal, lemongrass, lime leaves, garlic and chiles. Bring to a boil, reduce the heat, and simmer for 10 minutes.

Add the mushrooms, tomatoes, shrimp and spinach, and stir to combine. Cook for 3 minutes, then fold in the miso, lime juice, cilantro, honey, and apple juice. Serve immediately.

Tip

If shiitake mushrooms are not available, use clean button mushrooms, and include the stalks, or look for a nice mushroom selection box.

Lentil, couscous, and chili soup

Per serving

281 cals	4.1g fiber
3.5g fat	0.3g salt
0.5g saturated fat	
6g sugar	**0.7g fat per 100g**

I've been a fan of chunky soups ever since I converted to a mainly GI diet. This doesn't mean I'm averse to a smooth soup, it's just that these main-course soups fill you up and, for a meal, are relatively low in calories. This one is low GI, a good source of fiber and has a decent amount of beta-carotene. Serve with warm, seeded bread.

Serves 6

1 tablespoon olive oil
1 onion, roughly chopped
1 carrot, peeled and roughly chopped
1 stick of celery, finely sliced
3 garlic cloves, crushed to a paste
   with a little sea salt
1 tablespoon tomato paste
1 tablespoon rose harissa
2 teaspoons sweet paprika
½ teaspoon chili powder
1½ cups (11 oz) yellow lentils
¼ cup (2 oz) long grain rice
1 teaspoon ground cumin
½ teaspoon ground coriander
7 oz canned chopped tomatoes
2 quarts homemade vegetable stock
⅓ cup (2 oz) couscous, soaked in cold
   water for 10 minutes and drained
1 tablespoon chopped mint
1 tablespoon chopped cilantro
3 tablespoons chopped parsley
1 red pepper, finely sliced
2 scallions, finely sliced
2 tablespoons fat-free Greek yogurt

Heat the oil in a large saucepan over medium heat, and cook the onion, carrot, and celery for 8–10 minutes until softened, but not colored. Add the garlic, and cook for another 2 minutes.

Stir in the tomato paste, harissa, paprika, and chili powder, and cook, stirring constantly for 1 minute.

Add the lentils, rice, cumin, and coriander, and stir to combine, followed by the canned tomatoes and stock. Cover, bring to a boil, then reduce the temperature, and simmer for 35 minutes.

Ladle one-third of the soup into a blender and purée until smooth, then return to the pan and stir to combine. Add the couscous, 2 teaspoons of the mint, ½ tablespoon of the cilantro, and all the parsley. Return to the heat.

Meanwhile, combine the remaining herbs with the chili, scallions, and yogurt, season and mix well.

Serve the soup piping hot in warmed bowls with a floater of yogurt and a wedge of warm seeded bread.

A very quick no-cook pâté

Per serving

105 cals   0.5g fiber

2g fat   1.5g salt

0.6g saturated fat

2.4g sugar   **1.4g fat per 100g**

This pâté has lots of lovely flavors and is a good standby to have in the refrigerator for those munchy moments—all you need are a few knife skills. Serve with warm bread, crackers, or pita bread, the choice is yours.

Serves 4

1 cooked chicken or turkey breast, skin removed

4 oz lean cooked ham

6 button mushrooms, finely diced

4 cornichons (baby gherkins), finely diced

1 tablespoon Lilliput (baby) capers

2 shallots, finely diced

2 tablespoons chopped parsley

juice and grated zest of 1 unwaxed lemon

2 teaspoons anchovy sauce (optional)

1 teaspoon chopped tarragon

½ cup (4 oz) low-fat fromage frais

Finely chop the chicken and ham into small dice. You could use a food processor rather than a knife, but this tends to pulp the meat to a paste —I prefer a rougher texture.

Then it's really simple: just combine the meat with all the other ingredients and mix well. Allow the flavors to develop for one hour before seasoning.

Tip

You can use the same recipe to make a variety of fish pâtés: try using canned salmon (blend in a food processor), cooked shrimp (dice finely) or white crabmeat (no chopping or blending required, just mixing).

A textured bean pâté

Per serving

96 cals   2.7g fiber

1.5g fat   0.2g salt

0.4g saturated fat

3.8g sugar   **1.1g fat per 100g**

A cross between pâté and a dip, it's a useful kitchen cupboard basics standby that has a good balance of flavors.

Serves 6

1 floury potato, peeled and cut into ¾-inch dice

14 oz canned cannellini beans, drained and rinsed

2 garlic cloves, crushed to a paste with a little sea salt

2 teaspoons superfine sugar

3 tablespoons low-fat fromage frais

3 scallions, finely sliced

2 tomatoes, seeded and diced

8 basil leaves, roughly chopped

1 tablespoon sherry vinegar

1 hard-boiled egg, finely chopped

Place the diced potato into a pan of cold water with a little salt and bring to a boil. Simmer until tender, about 10 minutes, then add the drained beans to the pan to warm through. Drain and return to dry out over low heat.

Add the garlic, sugar, and fromage frais to the warm potato and bean mixture, and crush it with a potato masher, or more slowly with a fork. (It's important to add the wet ingredients while the potatoes are still warm so that they are more easily absorbed.)

Fold in the remaining ingredients, and season well. Serve with crackers, bruschetta, or crostini, or with warm pita breads.

Tip

There are many sorts of canned beans, all good, but white beans give this a better color.

Chicken satay with cucumber relish

Per stick

72 cals	0.2g fiber
1.4g fat	0.3g salt
0.8g saturated fat	
8.9g sugar	**1.7g fat per 100g**

There are not many who will turn down a satay stick; they are very addictive, but before you help yourself to a third or fourth, always take into consideration the total fat, not the fat per skewer. Peanuts are traditionally used in a satay sauce, but this version omits them, which considerably cuts the fat—and also has the advantage of making these skewers suitable for anyone with a nut allergy.

Makes 15 sticks

CHICKEN SATAY:

11 oz skinless chicken breast, cut
    into 15 thin strips
½ cup (4 fl oz) light coconut milk
2 tablespoons honey
1 tablespoon light soy sauce
4 tablespoons finely chopped cilantro,
    leaf, stalk and root (if available)
2 hot red peppers, finely diced
4 garlic cloves, mashed to a paste with
    a small amount of sea salt
1 teaspoon grated fresh ginger
½ teaspoon ground turmeric
½ teaspoon hot curry paste
lime wedges, to serve

CUCUMBER RELISH:

¾ cup (6 fl oz) rice or cider vinegar
6 tablespoons honey
1 cucumber, peeled, seeded and
    finely diced
2 teaspoons tamarind paste
3 tablespoons finely chopped cilantro
1 teaspoon finely chopped mint
2 mild red peppers, seeded and very
    finely sliced on the diagonal
1 teaspoon grated fresh ginger

To make the cucumber relish, bring the vinegar and honey to a boil in a non-reactive saucepan, reduce the heat and simmer for 10 minutes. Pour into a bowl, allow to cool, then fold in the remaining ingredients. To keep the cucumber green and tangy, make it no more than 1 hour before serving. If you want to make it the day before, the cucumber will lose its bright green color, but the flavors will be developed…you can't have it both ways.

For the satay, combine all the ingredients except the chicken in a bowl, then add the chicken and massage together until the meat is fully coated. Marinate in the refrigerator for up to 24 hours, but for no less than an hour.

To place on (pre-soaked) wooden skewers, weave the stick through the chicken in an "in and out" broad sewing movement, then stretch the chicken down the skewer, covering the sharp point with chicken to create a flat surface, top and bottom.

Place the skewers on a very lightly oiled, flat baking sheet, place under a hot broiler, cook for 3–4 minutes on each side, then serve with the relish, lime wedges, and for a main course, serve with plain boiled rice.

Phyllo beef rolls

Per serving

325 cals   5.2g fiber

7.3g fat   0.5g salt

2.1g saturated fat

30.3g sugar   **3g fat per 100g**

Not all of us have access to spring roll wrappers, but you can get a similar effect by using phyllo dough. The filling is simple, with a slight sweetness given by the fruits. Serve with a sweet chili dipping sauce and salad.

Serves 4

2 teaspoons olive oil

1 onion, finely chopped

2 garlic cloves, finely chopped

½ teaspoon ground cinnamon

2 teaspoons mint sauce

5 oz extra-lean ground beef

1 carrot, peeled and finely diced

1 leek, washed and finely diced

6 dried apricots, finely diced

⅓ cup (2 oz) golden raisins

⅓ cup (2 oz) dried cherries

8 sheets phyllo dough

spray of olive oil

Heat the oil in a frying pan, add the onion and garlic and cook over medium heat for 8–10 minutes. Stir in the cinnamon and mint sauce.

Add the ground beef to the onion, breaking up any lumps with the back of a spoon. Cook until brown, then add the carrot, leek, apricots, golden raisins, and dried cherries. Cook for 12 minutes until the carrots have softened slightly. Allow to cool for 10 minutes.

Preheat the oven to 400°F.

Lay one sheet of phyllo on your worktop and cut it in half crosswise. Spray one half with oil, turn it over and spray the other side; lay the other sheet on top and spray again. Lay one-eighth of the beef mixture along the edge of the phyllo closest to you, leaving a ½-inch border. Fold the ends over the beef, then roll up, making sure the ends are tucked in. Lay the roll, seam side down, on a flat baking sheet. Repeat the process with the other seven sheets of dough.

Bake for 12–15 minutes until golden, checking from time to time to make sure they are not burning.

Spiced vegetable fritters with mango chutney dip

Per serving
265 cals   2.5g fiber
3.1g fat   1.8g salt
0.4g saturated fat
16.2g sugar   **1g fat per 100g**

This Indian-influenced recipe comes from the same family as an onion bhaji, but has more flavor. We're not deep-frying here, so have no fear, just enjoy them when you're feeling hungry. They do reheat, although they are better cooked fresh.

Serves 4

1⅔ cups (5 oz) chickpea flour

1 teaspoon sea salt

½ cup (4 fl oz) water

½ teaspoon ground turmeric

½ teaspoon chili powder

½ teaspoon ground coriander

½ teaspoon ground cumin

½ teaspoon garam masala

2 garlic cloves, grated

1 onion, finely sliced

¼ butternut squash, peeled, seeded, and grated

1 zucchini, grated

3 new potatoes, grated

3 tablespoons chopped cilantro

2 teaspoons chopped mint

spray of vegetable oil

DIP:

3 tablespoons smooth mango chutney

4 tablespoons fat-free Greek yogurt

1 teaspoon chopped mint

Combine the flour, salt, and water in a bowl and beat until smooth. Add the spices and beat again.

Combine the vegetables in a bowl and mix well. Fold in the herbs, then pour in the batter and stir to combine.

Spray a large frying pan with vegetable oil, heat, then drop spoonfuls of vegetable batter into the pan, pushing them down to make flat, rough circles. Cook over medium heat for 4 minutes on each side. If you need to cook the fritters in batches, keep the others warm in a cool (150°F) oven.

Make the mango chutney dip by combining all the ingredients, and serve with the fritters.

Tip

There are all sorts of possibilities when it comes to vegetables to use—try a green fritter with broccoli, peas, and cooked, chopped spinach.

Bruschetta of roast peppers with chili, garlic, and parsley

Per serving

262 cals   4.4g fiber

5.1g fat   1.3g salt

0.8g saturated fat

13.2g sugar   **2g fat per 100g**

The topping can also be eaten as part of an antipasto spread, a salad, or folded through pasta. These wonderful, warm Mediterranean flavors are packed with antioxidants, especially vitamin C and beta-carotene.

Serves 4

4 red bell peppers

3 anchovy fillets, halved lengthwise and rinsed

¼ teaspoon crushed red pepper flakes

4 garlic cloves, thinly sliced

3 scallions, finely sliced

2 tablespoons chopped flat-leaf parsley

zest and juice of 1 organic orange

2 teaspoons Lilliput (baby) capers, drained and rinsed

2 teaspoons extra-virgin olive oil

1 ciabatta loaf, halved horizontally lengthwise, then each piece cut in half vertically to make 4 slices

Place the peppers over a gas flame, or on the highest shelf under a hot broiler. Keep turning with tongs, as each side becomes blackened and blistered. Place the peppers in a bowl, cover tightly with plastic wrap and leave for 20 minutes to steam in their own heat. When cool enough to handle, scrape off the blackened skin, remove the core and seeds, then cut the flesh into long thin strips.

Transfer the peppers together with any juices from the bowl to a clean bowl, and combine with the anchovies, red pepper flakes, garlic, scallions, parsley, orange zest and juice, and the capers. Season to taste.

Meanwhile, brush the ciabatta slices with a scant amount of olive oil, and toast the cut side under the broiler or on a griddle pan until golden. Divide the pepper mixture between the four slices and serve as a snack, or with a leafy salad.

Tip

To save time, buy yourself a jar of wood-roasted peppers, but as they're usually in olive oil, drain well and pat with paper towels. Unfortunately the canned peppers in brine have little or no flavor.

Spicy pea fritters with cilantro and potato raita

Per serving

302 cals	2.5g fiber
5.4g fat	0.5g salt
0.6g saturated fat	
6.5g sugar	**1.9g fat per 100g**

This dish is loosely inspired by Indian pakoras, which are usually deep-fried. In this case we lightly pan-fry the fritters with the merest hint of vegetable oil. They are extremely addictive, and work very well for a light lunch or as a snack to hand around with drinks.

Serves 4

2¾ cups (8 oz) chickpea flour

1 teaspoon baking soda

¾ cup (6 fl oz) water

2 teaspoons vegetable oil

1 small onion, roughly chopped

4 garlic cloves, roughly chopped

1 teaspoon ground turmeric

½ teaspoon ground cumin

½ teaspoon ground coriander

½ teaspoon ground fennel

½ teaspoon crushed red pepper flakes

2 teaspoons chopped mint

1 cup (5 oz) frozen green peas, defrosted

3 scallions, finely sliced

handful of arugula leaves, roughly chopped

spray of vegetable oil

RAITA:

1 cup (8 oz) fat-free Greek yogurt

6 oz cooked potato, cut into ½-inch dice

½ bunch of cilantro, roughly chopped

1 garlic clove, crushed to a paste with a little sea salt

½ teaspoon cumin seeds, toasted

Sift the chickpea flour and baking soda into a bowl with a pinch of salt. Whisk in the water to produce a smooth batter.

Meanwhile, heat the oil in a frying pan, and over medium heat, cook the onion and garlic for 8–10 minutes to soften them with no color. Add the spices, stir to combine, and cook for another minute. Allow to cool slightly, then pulse the mixture in a mini food processor until reasonably smooth.

Spoon the spiced onion into the batter, along with the mint, peas, scallions, and arugula. Allow the mixture to rest for 15 minutes to let the flavors develop.

Meanwhile, combine all the ingredients for the raita in a bowl, and leave for 30 minutes. Season to taste.

Preheat the oven to 325°F.

Spray a nonstick frying pan with vegetable oil, and warm over medium heat. Drop level tablespoonfuls of the pea batter into the pan, and flatten slightly. Cook for 3 minutes on each side, then place in the oven to keep warm while you cook the remainder in batches. Serve with the raita.

Tip

Have fun changing the content of the fritters, using different vegetables, or even oven-cooked chicken or shrimp.

Turkey and lettuce cups

Per serving

174 cals   1.2g fiber

6.7g fat   2.2g salt

2.4g saturated fat

6.8g sugar   **2.9g fat per 100g**

Every time we go out for a Chinese meal, these lettuce cups are always my kids' first choice. They are light, reasonably healthy, are packed full of flavor, and they're pretty quick to make.

Serves 4

2 teaspoons vegetable oil

2 teaspoons very finely shredded lemongrass, outside layers discarded

2 bird's eye chiles, seeded and finely sliced

3 garlic cloves, crushed to a paste with a little sea salt

1-inch piece of fresh ginger, peeled and finely grated, retaining any juice

10 oz ground turkey or chicken

½ cucumber, seeded and cut into ½-inch dice

¾ cup (2 oz) snow peas, trimmed, and cut into very thin strips

4 scallions, thinly sliced on the diagonal

3 canned water chestnuts, drained and cut into ¼-inch dice

8 basil leaves

handful of cilantro leaves

4 iceberg or little gem lettuce leaves

¼ cup (2 oz) bean sprouts, soaked in ice water, then drained just before use

DRESSING:

juice of 2 limes

1 tablespoon low-sodium soy sauce

1 tablespoon rice wine vinegar

2 tablespoons kecap manis (Indonesian soy sauce)

2 teaspoons honey

½ teaspoon chili oil

Heat a wok with the oil, then add the lemongrass, chiles, garlic, and ginger and cook for 2 minutes, stirring continuously. Remove and set aside.

Add the ground turkey or chicken to the wok, and cook over high heat, stirring continuously, and breaking up any lumps with a fork or spoon. Cook for about 4 minutes until brown.

Whisk together the dressing ingredients.

Return the lemongrass mixture to the wok, along with half the dressing, and toss thoroughly. Add the remaining ingredients, except for the bean sprouts and lettuce leaves, and stir-fry for 30 seconds. Slide into a bowl and serve with the remaining dressing.

Your fellow diners can then spoon the turkey into their lettuce "cups," top with bean sprouts, and roll up and enjoy the crunch.

Tip

To separate iceberg leaves without tearing them, place the lettuce core-side up on your cutting board, remove the core using a small sharp knife, then hit the lettuce hard on the bottom, which will help to loosen the leaves.

Curried eggplant purée

Per serving

86 cals   3.5g fiber
3.2g fat   0.2g salt
0.5g saturated fat
8g sugar   **1.3g fat per 100g**

I know that eggplant is not everyone's cup of tea, but I am a bit of a fan as I find them wonderful vehicles for absorbing some fab flavors. This dish, as well as being a great vegetable side, also doubles up as a dip, or you can serve it with rice.

Serves 6

2 large eggplants
1 tablespoon vegetable oil
2 onions, finely chopped
2 garlic cloves, crushed to a paste
    with a little sea salt
2 teaspoons grated fresh ginger
2 chiles, finely diced
2 cardamom pods, lightly crushed
½ teaspoon ground cumin
½ teaspoon ground coriander
¼ teaspoon ground fennel
½ teaspoon ground turmeric
½ teaspoon freshly ground black pepper
1 cup (8 oz) fat-free Greek yogurt
1 teaspoon garam masala
3 tomatoes, roughly chopped
2 tablespoons chopped cilantro

Preheat the oven to 375°F.

Place the eggplants on a rack in the oven, and cook until very soft and almost collapsed, about 40–45 minutes.

Meanwhile, heat the oil in a large saucepan, and cook the onions with the garlic, ginger, and chiles over low heat for 10–12 minutes. Add all the spices except for the garam masala, and cook for another 3–4 minutes.

When the eggplant is cooked, cut them in half lengthwise, and scoop out all the flesh, discarding the skins. Chop the flesh, add to the onion-spice mixture, and cook gently for 5 minutes. Add the yogurt, bring to a boil, then reduce the heat, and cook for 8 minutes, stirring frequently.

Finally, fold in the garam masala, tomatoes and chopped cilantro, cook for 3 minutes, and check the seasoning.

Baked herby tomatoes on rye toast

Per serving

220 cals   4g fiber
4.5g fat   1.8g salt
0.7g saturated fat
6.4g sugar   **1.9g fat per 100g**

Serves 4

6 ripe but firm large tomatoes, cut in half
½ teaspoon salt
2 shallots, peeled and roughly chopped
2 garlic cloves, roughly chopped
1 teaspoon thyme leaves
2 anchovy fillets, drained and roughly chopped
2 tablespoons chopped parsley
2 teaspoons snipped chives
½ teaspoon crushed red pepper flakes
2 cups (3 oz) fresh white bread crumbs
1 teaspoon extra-virgin olive oil
4 slices of rye toast

Carefully remove most of the seeds from the tomatoes with a teaspoon or melon baller. Sprinkle the cut sides with salt, and place cut-side down on paper towels to remove some of the liquid. Leave to stand for 20 minutes.

Preheat the oven to 400°F.

Place the shallots in a food processor with the garlic, thyme, anchovies, parsley, chives, chili flakes, bread crumbs, and oil, and pulse until well-combined, but not a paste. Season to taste.

Spoon the mixture into the tomato cavities, mounding it high, then bake in the oven for 20–25 minutes. Keep an eye on them for signs of burning, and turn the oven temperature down if necessary.

Serve the tomatoes on the rye toast.

Falafel

Per serving (based on 8 servings)
122 cals
2.4g fat
0.3g saturated fat
3g sugar

3.1g fiber
1g salt

2g fat per 100g

These can be made using canned chickpeas, but the texture will not be the same as when using dried. Falafel are normally deep-fried, but in the interests of a low-fat diet, you can pan-fry them in a small amount of oil.

Serves 6–8

2 cups (14 oz) dried chickpeas, soaked overnight in plenty of cold water

1 onion, roughly chopped

3 garlic cloves, roughly chopped

2 tablespoons chopped parsley

1 tablespoon chopped cilantro

1 teaspoon ground cumin

½ teaspoon ground fennel

1 teaspoon baking soda

2 tablespoons flour

1 teaspoon sea salt

spray of oil

YOGURT DIP:

1 cup (8 oz) fat-free Greek yogurt

1 tablespoon chopped mint

1 tablespoon sesame seeds, toasted

1 teaspoon mashed garlic

To make the dip, combine all the ingredients and leave for half an hour for the flavors to develop.

Meanwhile, place the soaked, drained chickpeas with the onion, garlic, herbs, and spices in a food processor, and pulse until almost smooth. Tip into a bowl, then add the baking soda, flour, and salt, and mix well. Turn onto a floured surface and knead for 5 minutes. Place the mixture on some plastic wrap and roll up like a sausage, about ¾-inch in diameter. Leave to rest in the refrigerator for 30 minutes.

Cut the falafel "sausage" into ½-inch discs.

Spray the oil into a frying pan and cook the falafel disks in batches over medium heat for 2 minutes on each side. Keep warm in the oven, then serve with the yogurt dip.

Two dips

Per serving (based on 6 servings)
57 cals / 40 cals
0.8g fat / 0.2g
0.4g saturated fat / 0g
5.5g sugar / 2.9g
1.1g fiber / 0.5g
0.6g salt / 0.2g
0.5g / 0.2g fat per 100g

These dips, to accompany crackers or crudité vegetables, are made using plenty of ingredients normally kept on hand. Each makes roughly 2½ cups.

CHILI AND RED PEPPER:

3 roasted peppers from a jar, drained well and patted dry

1 onion, finely chopped

2 tablespoons pickled jalapeño peppers from a jar, drained and chopped

6 basil leaves, finely chopped

7 oz canned chopped tomatoes

1 teaspoon tomato paste

1 cup (8 oz) low-fat cottage cheese

Combine all the ingredients except for the cheese in a blender or food processor, and blend until smooth. Fold the purée into the cottage cheese and it's ready.

SPICED SPINACH AND YOGURT:

⅔ cup (4 oz) frozen chopped spinach, drained and squeezed dry

2 garlic cloves, crushed to a paste with a little sea salt

1 teaspoon ground cumin

½ teaspoon ground turmeric

1 teaspoon hot or mild curry paste

2 scallions, finely chopped

2 teaspoons lemon juice

1¾ cups (14 oz) fat-free Greek yogurt

Combine all the ingredients, check the seasoning, and serve.

Per serving
198 cals
2.8g fat
1.1g saturated fat
4.9g sugar
2.5g fiber
1.8g salt
2.2g fat per 100g

Potato, tomato, and basil rolls

This recipe is multipurpose, I bake them in muffin pans, but you could make it into one loaf or even pan-fry patties.

Makes 8

7 oz floury potato, peeled and cut into ½-inch cubes

2 tablespoons low-fat spread

2⅓ cups (11 oz) self-rising flour

1 cup (8 fl oz) skim milk

1 roasted red pepper from a jar, drained and diced

⅓ cup (3 oz) sun-dried tomatoes, chopped

12 basil leaves, roughly chopped

½ cup (2 oz) reduced-fat mozzarella, grated

In a pan of boiling, salted water, cook the potatoes for about 10 minutes until tender, then drain and return to the hot pan to dry out slightly.

Meanwhile, preheat the oven to 400°F.

Mash the potato with the low-fat spread, then sift in the flour, and mix to combine. Stir in the milk, and fold in the red pepper, tomatoes, basil, and cheese.

Line 8 muffin pan holes with a disc of baking parchment, spoon in the mixture and smooth over or leave rustic. Brush the surface with milk, and bake in the oven for about 25–30 minutes. To test if ready, take one out and tap the base, which should sound hollow. Turn out onto wire racks to cool.

That taco moment

Per serving

156 cals 2.3g fiber
5.8g fat 0.9g salt
2.4g saturated fat
4.5g sugar **2.5g fat per 100g**

A favorite with young people, it's good to have youthful moments, and these are simple and tasty. Usually served with ground beef, I've reduced the fat by using turkey.

Makes 8

spray of olive oil
2 garlic cloves, crushed to a paste
  with a little sea salt
1 small onion, finely chopped
7 oz ground turkey
1 teaspoon chili powder
½ teaspoon ground cumin
½ teaspoon ground coriander
2½ cups (21 oz) canned red kidney
  beans, drained and rinsed
2 tablespoons tomato paste
1¼ cups (10 fl oz) chicken stock
7 oz canned chopped tomatoes
8 taco shells
½ small iceberg lettuce, shredded
  finely

SALSA:

½ cucumber, seeded and
  finely sliced
1 small red onion, finely diced
2 tomatoes, seeded and diced
1 tablespoon chopped cilantro
juice of 2 limes
2 teaspoons sweet chili sauce

Preheat the oven to 325°F.

Spray a little oil into a frying pan and cook the garlic, onion, and ground turkey until golden brown, breaking up any lumps with a wooden spoon.

Add the chili powder, cumin, ground coriander, kidney beans, tomato paste, and stock, and bring to a boil. Reduce the heat and simmer for 20 minutes, until the liquid reduces considerably. Fold in the tomatoes and season.

Meanwhile, make the salsa by combining all the ingredients, and warm the taco shells in the oven for 6–7 minutes.

Place the taco shells, turkey mixture, lettuce and salsa on the table for your diners to assemble themselves.

Tip

A dollop of fat-free Greek yogurt on top of each taco gives a creamy, cooling effect.

Honey-glazed chicken drumsticks

Per serving
182 cals   1.2g fiber
5.2g fat   0.9g salt
1g saturated fat
11.8g sugar   **2.4g fat per 100g**

This is one to have ready for when you have those hunger pangs. The steamed drumsticks can be prepared in advance, and then simply tossed with the other ingredients when you fancy a nibble. They can be eaten hot or cold.

Serves 4

8 skinless chicken drumsticks
2 teaspoons vegetable oil
1 onion, cut into 8 wedges
3 tomatoes, roughly chopped
2 tablespoons honey
½ teaspoon garlic salt
½ teaspoon chili powder
2 teaspoons curry paste (hot or mild...
   your choice)

Using a Chinese bamboo steamer set over a wok, or an electric tiered steamer, steam the drumsticks for 20 minutes.

Heat the oil in a wok or frying pan, then add the onion wedges and cook over medium heat for 12–15 minutes, then add the tomatoes, honey, garlic salt, chili powder, and curry paste. Stir to combine, then cook gently for 3 minutes to blend all the ingredients.

Add the drumsticks, and cook, turning continuously, for 4–5 minutes (if the drumsticks are hot from the steamer), until you build up a shiny glaze.

Tip

If glazing the chicken from cold, add a little water to the honey mixture to prevent it from burning, and cook the chicken for 15 minutes. As the chicken heats up, the water will evaporate, leaving the honey glaze intact.

Per serving
92 cals   1.1g fiber
2.3g fat   0.9g salt
0.7g saturated fat
13.2g sugar   **2g fat per 100g**

Prosciutto and nectarine skewers

This is a yummy little snack that takes no time to put together. If you're having friends over, make a few more and serve with drinks. They taste nice with a leafy salad, too.

Serves 4

4 slices prosciutto (Parma or
   Serrano ham)
4 nectarines, quartered and pitted
1 tablespoon dark brown sugar
¼ teaspoon ground allspice
16 mint leaves

Lay the prosciutto slices on your work surface and cut each lengthwise into four. Arrange the nectarine quarters, sideways, at one end of each sliver of ham.

Combine the sugar with the allspice, and sprinkle a little over the nectarine slices. Top each with a mint leaf, then roll up in the ham. Thread four onto a skewer (pre-soaked if wooden), and place under a hot broiler, turning from time to time until the prosciutto is crisp.

Serve hot, but warn your fellow diners.

Per serving			**Per serving**			**Per serving**	
57 cals	1.9g fiber		31 cals	1.5g fiber		24 cals	0.8g fiber
2.1g fat	0.9g salt		0.2g fat	0.8g salt		0.3g fat	0.4g salt
0.4g sat fat			0.1g sat fat			0g sat fat	
6.6g sugar	**1.1g fat per 100g**		6.6g sugar	**0.2g fat per 100g**		4.9g sugar	**0.5g fat per 100g**

Three simple salsas

Three flavor-filled salsas to accompany plain-cooked food, whether it's fish, chicken, pork, or beef.

SWEET RED SALSA:

Serves 4

4 roasted red bell peppers from a jar, drained and roughly chopped

½ red onion, finely diced

3 ripe tomatoes, seeded and diced

1 red pepper, seeded and finely sliced

2 garlic cloves, crushed to a paste with a little sea salt

⅛ teaspoon sweet paprika

2 teaspoons rose harissa

2 teaspoons extra-virgin olive oil

1 teaspoon red wine vinegar

Combine all the ingredients, check the seasoning, and serve at room temperature.

ASIAN CRUNCH SALSA:

Serves 4

¼ cucumber, peeled, seeded and finely diced

4 scallions, thinly sliced

1 mango, peeled, pitted, and finely diced

6 radishes, roughly diced

1 red pepper, seeded and finely diced

2 bamboo shoots, finely diced

½ teaspoon grated fresh ginger

grated zest and juice of 1 lime

1 tablespoon kecap manis (Indonesian soy sauce)

½ teaspoon nam pla (fish sauce)

2 teaspoons chopped mint

Combine all the ingredients, check the seasoning, and serve chilled.

JAMAICAN CHILI FIRE:

Serves 4

¼ pineapple, peeled, cored and diced

½ red bell pepper, seeded and diced

3 scallions, finely sliced

½ teaspoon chopped thyme

1 hot chile, seeded and finely diced

½ teaspoon ground cinnamon

1 garlic clove, crushed to a paste with a little sea salt

1 teaspoon sweet chili sauce

2 teaspoons chopped cilantro

½ teaspoon store-bought jerk paste

Combine all the ingredients, check the seasoning, and serve chilled.

Chinese pork in lettuce leaves

Per serving
195 cals
6.1g fat
2.1g saturated fat
3.4g sugar

1.1g fiber
2.4g salt

2.8g fat per 100g

This recipe is dedicated to my children, who love to eat it at our local Chinese restaurant—very habit-forming food that's ready in an instant, and has smack-in-the-mouth flavors.

Serves 4

1 teaspoon sesame oil
1 small onion, finely chopped
1 teaspoon garlic paste
1 teaspoon ginger paste
1 medium red chili, finely diced
11½ oz extra lean ground pork
2 tablespoons mirin (rice wine)
½ cup (3 oz) button mushrooms, finely chopped
2 tablespoons kecap manis (see page 86)
2 tablespoons oyster sauce
juice of 1 lime
½ cup (2 oz) bean sprouts
4 scallions, finely sliced
1 teaspoon chopped mint
1 tablespoon chopped cilantro
12 iceberg lettuce leaves

Heat the sesame oil in a wok, then add the onion, garlic, ginger, and chili, and stir briskly for 3 minutes. Add the pork, break up any lumps with the back of a spoon, and cook until just brown.

Add the mirin, mushrooms, kecap manis, oyster sauce, and lime juice, and stir to combine. Quickly fold in the bean sprouts, scallions, and herbs, and check the seasoning.

Serve with lettuce leaves, for your fellow diners to create their own lettuce wraps.

A neat little salad with color

Per serving
121 cals
4g fat
0.8g saturated fat
9.2g sugar

2.3g fiber
0.8g salt

2.5g fat per 100g

Anything brightly colored that jumps off the plate appears to taste better, and loads of color is excellent for different health benefits. This salad is made in a flash and both looks and tastes beautiful.

Serves 4

juice of 2 limes and grated zest of 1 lime
2 teaspoons nam pla (fish sauce)
1 teaspoon superfine sugar
1 medium-size ripe, but firm mango, peeled and roughly chopped
1 medium red onion, finely sliced
½ avocado, peeled and cut into ¼-inch dice
4 cherry tomatoes, halved
1 medium-heat green chili, seeded and finely diced
6 mint leaves, roughly chopped
½ small bunch of cilantro, leaves only
7 oz canned tuna in spring water, drained and flaked

Combine the lime juice and zest, nam pla, and sugar in a bowl, and stir until the sugar has dissolved.

In a separate bowl, combine the mango, onion, avocado, tomatoes, and chili. Pour over enough dressing to coat, dress on four plates, then scatter with mint, cilantro and tuna flakes.

Vegetarian rice paper rolls

Per serving

39 cals	0.6g fiber
0.2g fat	0.7g salt
0g saturated fat	
2.8g sugar	**0.5g fat per 100g**

These are all about crunch, texture, and flavor. They make a lovely snack, or something to serve with drinks, and the possible fillings are numerous and not just vegetarian —shreds of cooked chicken, salmon, or shrimp would all work well.

Makes 12

1 red bell pepper, seeded and cut into julienne (thin strips)

1 small can sliced bamboo shoots, cut into julienne

4 canned hearts of palm, cut into julienne

½ cup (2 oz) bean sprouts

12 mint leaves, shredded

½ bunch of cllantro, roughly chopped

12 rice paper squares (9½ x 7 inches)

SAUCE:

2 garlic cloves, crushed to a paste with a little sea salt

1 tablespoon nam pla (fish sauce)

juice of 2 limes

2 tablespoons oyster sauce

3 teaspoons honey

2 teaspoons hot chili sauce

Combine the first six ingredients in a bowl. In a separate bowl combine all the ingredients for the sauce.

Pour some warm water into another bowl and, working one at a time, dip a rice paper square into the water to soften, then place it on your work surface, and pat it dry with paper towels.

To make up the roll, place the rice paper in front of you, in a diamond position, then arrange a small amount of the filling across the paper, with some sticking out at one end. Drizzle the vegetables with a little sauce, then roll up, tucking in one end, but leaving one end open. Repeat with the remaining rice paper squares.

Light lunches
and suppers

Basic pizza dough

Per serving

450 cals	4g fiber
2g fat	1.3g salt
0.3g saturated fat	
2.6g sugar	**1g fat per 100g**

This is a basic recipe that will be useful for all sorts of toppings that can be low in fat. We normally associate cheese with pizza, but there are some delicious toppings you can use to avoid the high fat content.

Makes 4 bases

¼ oz fresh yeast, or 1 teaspoon active
   dry yeast
½ teaspoon superfine sugar
4½ cups (18 oz) all-purpose flour,
   plus extra for dusting
1⅔ cups (13 fl oz) lukewarm water
1 teaspoon sea salt
spray of olive oil

For your starter dough, dissolve the yeast with the sugar plus 2 tablespoons of the flour in ¼ cup of the warm water. Leave for 5 minutes until it starts bubbling, then add the remaining water.

Add the salt and half the remaining flour, and stir with your hand to form a paste. Gradually add the remaining flour until you have pliable dough. Shape into a ball, and put into a bowl that you've sprayed with a little olive oil. Cover with plastic wrap, and leave in a warm place for 10 minutes.

Tip the dough onto a floured surface and knead with the heel of your hand for about 10 minutes until springy, smooth, and elastic. Cut the dough into four equal parts, roll into balls and place on a lightly oil-sprayed flat tray, keeping each ball well apart. Cover with a damp dish towel and leave in a warm place for 1 hour to rise.

A good tip for shaping the pizza base is to use the metal base of a loose-bottomed 9-inch cake or tart pan. Push down the dough onto the well-floured pan and, with your fingertips, spread the dough until it fills the base, leaving the edge slightly thicker. You can then place the pizza base onto a flat, floured baking sheet before arranging or spooning on a topping.

Basic tomato, oregano, and garlic topping

Per serving	
(including pizza base)	
499 cals	4.4g fiber
4.7g fat	3g salt
0.7g saturated fat	
5.1g sugar	**1.8g fat per 100g**

This is the simplest of toppings that you can add to or alter, for example, by substituting basil for the oregano. Don't be tempted to use fresh oregano as the dried has a more genuine pizza taste, and won't go black when cooked. Tomatoes are a great source of vitamin K and also contain lycopene, which is an excellent antioxidant.

Makes topping for 4 bases

scant cup (7 fl oz) tomato sauce

½ teaspoon dried oregano

¼ teaspoon crushed red pepper flakes

3 garlic cloves, crushed to a paste
    with a little sea salt

½ teaspoon freshly ground
    black pepper

8 anchovy fillets, rinsed, dried, and
    cut in half lengthwise

16 pitted Kalamata olives in brine,
    rinsed and halved

1 teaspoon extra-virgin olive oil

1 quantity of Basic Pizza Dough
    (see page 93)

Preheat the oven to 475°F, then place a flat baking sheet in the oven to become extremely hot.

Meanwhile, make the topping sauce by combining the first five ingredients.

Remove the hot baking sheet from the oven, flour it generously and put on one or two bases, depending on their size. Spoon 2–3 tablespoons of the tomato sauce over the pizza base, leaving a ½-inch border.

Arrange the slices of anchovy over the tomato sauce, then scatter each pizza with 8 olive halves. Brush the border with a thick coating of olive oil.

Bake in the preheated oven for 8 minutes until crisp. Serve with a leafy salad.

Tip

Unless you have two large baking sheets, you may have to cook the pizzas individually or in two batches. And if you wish, you could use pickled anchovies instead of the ones preserved in oil.

Mini carrot "cakes" with dried fruit

Per serving

201 cals   7.3g fiber

1.6g fat   0.6g salt

0.3g saturated fat

26.5g sugar   **0.5g fat per 100g**

These cakes-cum-burgers have been a favorite of mine for many a year. They have loads of flavor, with a lovely sweetness, and can be served as a vegetable side dish, or as a light lunch served with salad.

Serves 4

10 medium carrots, cooked until soft, and drained

6 tablespoons white bread crumbs

6 dried apricots, finely diced

2 teaspoons chopped golden raisins

4 scallions, finely diced

4 garlic cloves, finely chopped

1 teaspoon crushed red pepper flakes

2 teaspoons grated orange zest

1 egg white

6 tablespoons mixed chopped parsley, mint, and dill

flour, for coating

spray of vegetable oil, for frying

1 red onion, finely sliced

cilantro leaves

Mash the carrots, then add the remaining ingredients up to the flour, and season. Knead the mixture well; if it's too wet, add more bread crumbs—the mixture should be soft and slightly damp.

Mold the purée into four "burgers" roughly 2 inches in diameter, coating your hands with flour to prevent the mixture sticking.

Dredge each cake in flour, then spray a nonstick frying pan with oil and cook the cakes gently until brown on both sides.

Serve with the finely sliced red onion and cilantro leaves, as well as the yogurt dip described below.

Tip

Make sure the cooked carrots are really dry before mashing.

Herbed yogurt dip

Per serving

27 cals   0g fiber

0g fat   0.1g salt

0g saturated fat

2g sugar   **0g fat per 100g**

This dip is based on an Indian raita and goes really well with these carrot cakes and plain grilled fish.

Serves 4

scant cup (7 oz) fat-free Greek yogurt

1 garlic clove, finely chopped

1 tablespoon chopped cilantro

2 teaspoons chopped mint

¼ teaspoon ground black pepper

Combine all the ingredients together in a large bowl. Leave the flavors to develop for 1 hour before serving.

Season with sea salt just before eating.

Shrimp tabbouleh baked potatoes

Per serving
254 cals   3.6g fiber
3.8g fat   0.4g salt
0.5g saturated fat
3.3g sugar   **1.3g fat per 100g**

Made correctly, tabbouleh is a wonderful dish; it's when it's all grain and no green that it becomes a let-down. I've tried it here with baked potatoes, which are a great source of carbohydrate and fiber, and their hot fluffiness is an excellent marriage for the greens.

Serves 4

4 medium baking potatoes, washed
⅓ cup (2 oz) bulgur (cracked wheat)
1½ cups (2 oz) flat-leaf parsley, leaves only, finely chopped
½ bunch of mint, leaves only, chopped
3 scallions, thinly sliced
1 tomato, seeded and diced
½ teaspoon ground cumin
1 tablespoon extra-virgin olive oil
juice and grated zest of 1 unwaxed lemon
2 oz cooked shrimp
2 tablespoons fat-free Greek yogurt
pinch of smoked paprika

Preheat the oven to 425°F.

Place the potatoes on a rack over a baking sheet in the oven. Bake for 20 minutes, then reduce the heat to 350°F and bake for another 50 minutes.

Meanwhile, soak the bulgur wheat in cold water for 12–15 minutes, then drain and squeeze dry. Put in a bowl with the remaining ingredients except the yogurt and paprika. Mix to combine and season well.

Cut a large cross in the top of each potato, squeeze the sides to open the cross, and top with the tabbouleh. Serve any extra on the side. Top with a dollop of yogurt, and a sprinkling of paprika.

Tip

This may seem like a long cooking time for the potato, but I like my centers really fluffy, and the skins really crispy.

Cold oysters with spicy apple salsa

Per serving
(based on 24)
12 cals   0.2g fiber
0.1g fat   0.3g salt
0g saturated fat
1.2g sugar   **0.5g fat per 100g**

This salsa also works with cooked oysters, cooked mussels and grilled fish.

Makes 24

24 raw oysters, opened on the half shell
2 teaspoons honey
1 tablespoon nam pla (fish sauce)
juice of 2 limes and the grated zest of 1 lime
1 hot red pepper, seeded and finely diced
½ cucumber, peeled, seeded and finely diced
1 Granny Smith apple, peeled and diced
2 scallions, finely chopped
15 mint leaves, finely chopped

Place the oysters on a bed of ice.

Combine the remaining ingredients, check the seasoning, then spoon over the oysters half an hour before eating.

White bean, shrimp, and arugula salad

Per serving

130 cals   3.6g fiber
3.7g fat   0.9g salt
0.7g saturated fat
4.3g sugar   **1.9g fat per 100g**

Beans are a great source of fiber, and this salad mixes protein with carbs to help fill you up. A very quick salad to produce, this makes a lovely light lunch, served with warm, seeded bread.

Serves 4

14 oz canned cannellini beans, drained
1 tablespoon extra-virgin olive oil
juice and zest of 1 unwaxed lemon
1 teaspoon honey
½ teaspoon black pepper
1 mild long red chili, seeded and
    finely chopped
1 garlic clove, crushed to a paste with
    a little sea salt
1 red onion, thinly sliced
1 stick celery, thinly sliced
6 button mushrooms, thinly sliced
16 cooked jumbo shrimp, peeled
2 handfuls of arugula leaves

Heat the beans with a little salted water for 3 minutes, drain, then tip into a bowl. While still warm, combine the beans with the olive oil, lemon juice and zest, honey, pepper, and chili. Allow to cool, then combine with the remaining ingredients.

Tip

Feel free to change the beans to green kidney (flageolet), borlotti or kidney, the shrimp to cooked skinless chicken, and the arugula to watercress or Belgian endive.

Teriyaki beef and mango kabobs

Per serving

499 cals   1.4g fiber
10.2g fat   3.1g salt
3.7g saturated fat
6.8g sugar   **2.7g fat per 100g**

The sweetness of this teriyaki marinade is always a delicious treat. Serve with salad, rice, or green vegetables.

Serves 4

1 lb sirloin steaks, fat removed
1 mango cut into ¾-inch chunks
4 scallions, each cut into ¾-inch pieces
spray of vegetable oil
4 cups cooked rice, to serve (1¼ cups raw)

FOR THE MARINADE:

2 teaspoons cornstarch
3 tablespoons sake or dry sherry
2 tablespoons rice vinegar
4 tablespoons kecap manis (see page 86)
2 garlic cloves, crushed to a paste with a
    little sea salt
½ teaspoon grated fresh ginger

First start by making the marinade. Stir everything together and tip into a shallow dish.

Beat the steaks until very thin, and cut into strips, then place in the marinade, and leave for at least 2 hours.

Thread four pieces of each (beef, mango and scallion) alternately on four, pre-soaked wooden skewers. The best way to secure the steak on the skewers is to weave the skewers in and out of the steak.

Heat the marinade in a small saucepan until hot, stirring from time to time.

Spray a large frying pan with vegetable oil until smoking, then place the skewers in the pan and cook for 1–3 minutes on each side, depending on how rare you like your meat. While the kabobs are cooking, baste frequently with the sauce.

A Spanish tortilla

Per serving
(based on 4 servings)
294 cals   5.6g fiber
8.7g fat   1.2g salt
2.2g saturated fat
4.6g sugar   **2.8g fat per 100g**

Tortilla, frittata, Spanish omelet, what's in a name? All are variations on the same theme, though of course a Spanish omelet IS a tortilla. This slow-cooked, deep-set omelet is delicious served at room temperature with a hunk of bread and a salad. Lots of protein, with a smattering of iron, vitamin A, and a healthy dose of fiber, all make you feel really worthy. A great one for your lunchbox.

Serves 4–6

2 teaspoons olive oil

4 scallions, finely sliced

1 zucchini, cut into ½-inch dice

½ cup (3 oz) frozen baby fava or lima beans, defrosted

½ cup (3 oz) frozen peas, defrosted

5 oz cooked new potatoes, sliced

3 whole free-range eggs

3 egg whites

4 basil leaves, shredded

TO SERVE:

mixed salad leaves

4 thick slices of warm, crusty whole grain bread

Heat the oil in a 9-inch nonstick, curved-sided frying pan until really smoking. Add the scallions and zucchini, and cook over medium heat for 6–8 minutes. Tip into a bowl and set aside.

Meanwhile, heat a small pan of salted water to boiling, then add the fava beans and cook for 3 minutes. Drain, refresh, and remove the leathery outer skin to reveal the emerald jewel-colored vegetables. Combine these with the peas and new potatoes and add to the scallions and zucchini.

Beat the whole eggs with the egg whites and fold into the vegetables. Add the basil and season.

Turn your broiler on to high. Heat the curved-sided frying pan over low heat, then tip in the omelet mixture and flatten gently to submerge the vegetables. Cook over low heat for 8–10 minutes, then place under the hot broiler for about 2 minutes, allowing the omelet to cook slightly before sliding it onto a flat plate.

Serve the tortilla while still slightly warm, or at room temperature with the mixed salad, and warm crusty bread.

Grilled polenta with wild mushrooms, bacon, and thyme

Per serving
278 cals   0.9g fiber
6g fat   3.9g salt
1.4g saturated fat
1.3g sugar   **1.6g fat per 100g**

When did you last eat grilled polenta? It was fashionable for a few years, then disappeared, which was a pity, because it makes a great base for so many toppings, and for those with gluten intolerances, it makes a good substitute for bruschetta. Tastes good with a dollop of fat-free Greek yogurt.

Serves 4

30 fl oz vegetable or chicken stock
8 oz instant dried polenta
spray of olive oil
1 tablespoon olive oil
2 slices Canadian bacon, fat removed, cut into small strips
2 shallots, finely chopped
4 sprigs of thyme
3 garlic cloves, peeled and mashed to a paste with a little sea salt
8 oz mixed wild mushrooms (I like ceps, girolles and shiitakes), sliced if large
1 tablespoon snipped chives

Bring the stock to a boil, in a saucepan, then pour in the polenta in a slow, steady trickle while you stir vigorously with a wooden spoon. Cook over medium heat until the polenta starts to come away from the sides of the saucepan, about 5 minutes. Season generously.

Pour the polenta onto a lightly oil-sprayed, nonstick, shallow baking pan, and spread it with the back of a wet spoon or offset spatula until smooth and about 1 inch thick. Leave to cool and thicken.

When the polenta has cooled, cut it into rectangles. (You may have more polenta than you need, but the leftovers can be cut into croûtons for soup.) Lightly spray a nonstick grill pan with oil and heat over medium heat until very hot. Cook the polenta rectangles until nicely marked on both sides, about 4 minutes.

Meanwhile, heat the olive oil in a nonstick frying pan, add the bacon and cook for 3 minutes. Add the shallots, thyme, and garlic, and stir to combine.

Increase the heat, and stir in the mushrooms, then fry fiercely for about 2 minutes, stirring continuously. Season, then add the chives and spoon on top of the grilled polenta. Serve very hot.

Tip

Got a problem finding wild mushrooms? Never fear, just buy field or oyster mushrooms, slice them up, and cook in the same way.

Thai fish cakes with cucumber dipping sauce

Per serving

242 cals   0.9g fiber
3.8g fat   2.9g salt
0.5g saturated fat
18.3g sugar   **1g fat per 100g**

These fish cakes have a much denser texture than the average British potato-based cakes, and because of this, you should use only white filleted fish. By choice, I go for red snapper, which is really meaty and blends to a smooth paste. The fish cakes go well with a warm, crunchy salad.

Serves 4

18 oz red snapper fillets, cut into 1-inch pieces
2 tablespoons red curry paste
3 fresh kaffir lime leaves, central spine
   removed
3 scallions, finely sliced
½ piece of fresh ginger, peeled and grated
1 egg white
1 tablespoon nam pla (fish sauce)
juice and zest of 1 lime
3 tablespoons cilantro leaves, roughly chopped
¼ cup (1½ oz) extra fine green beans, very
   finely sliced
¼ cup (2 oz) corn kernels (canned or frozen)
1 bird's eye chile, seeded and finely
   chopped
spray of vegetable oil

CUCUMBER DIPPING SAUCE:

½ cucumber, seeded and cut into ¼-inch dice
½ teaspoon sea salt
¼ cup (2 oz) superfine sugar
½ cup (4 fl oz) mirin (Japanese rice wine)
½ cup (4 fl oz) water
½ cup (4 fl oz) rice vinegar
½ tablespoon grated fresh ginger
1 tablespoon nam pla (fish sauce)
2 bird's eye chiles, finely chopped
2 scallions, finely sliced
2 tablespoons chopped cilantro
1 tablespoon chopped mint

For the dipping sauce, sprinkle the cucumber with a little salt in a sieve or colander, and toss to combine, then leave for 20 minutes before rinsing.

Heat the sugar, mirin, water, vinegar, and ginger in a saucepan, and stir until the sugar dissolves. Cool, then pour over the cucumber in the bowl. Fold in the remaining ingredients, then refrigerate until ready to use.

For the fish cakes, put the fish, curry paste, lime leaves, scallions, ginger, egg white, nam pla, lime juice and zest into a food processor, and blend until smooth. Spoon into a bowl, then fold in the remaining ingredients, except the oil.

With wet hands, roll the fish paste into small balls, then flatten into smooth cakes. You should produce about 16 fish cakes altogether.

Spray the cakes top and bottom with the oil. Heat a large frying pan, preferably nonstick, and cook the fish cakes in batches for 3 minutes on each side until golden. Keep warm in a cool oven while you cook the rest.

Serve with the cucumber dipping sauce.

Tip

If you can't find red snapper, pollock works well, is sustainable, and is good value.

Baked sweet potato with sea bass ceviche

Per serving
334 cals   6.8g fiber
3.9g fat   0.4g salt
0.7g saturated fat
19.7g sugar   **0.7g fat per 100g**

A cracking dish for summer or winter, with contrasting textures and temperatures. The lime juice "cooks" the sea bass by marination; the longer you leave it in the marinade, the more it will cook. If you're a fan of sashimi, dress the fish just before serving.

Serves 2

2 sweet potatoes (approx. 14 oz), halved and washed, skin on

1 medium-heat chile, seeded and very thinly sliced

½ red onion, very finely sliced

6 radishes, trimmed and very thinly sliced

1 large, vine-ripened tomato, seeded and cut into small dice

½ cucumber, seeded and cut into small dice

juice of 2 limes

2 teaspoons canola oil

1 teaspoon superfine sugar

8 oz skinless sea bass fillet

½ bunch of cilantro, leaves and stems roughly chopped

Preheat the oven to 400°F.

Place the sweet potato halves on a rack in the oven and bake for 40 minutes, or until tender.

In a bowl or dish, combine the chili, red onion, radishes, tomato, cucumber, lime juice, oil, and sugar. Leave for 15 minutes, stirring from time to time.

Depending on how you like your fish "cooked," cut the sea bass into thin strips or thicker batons, and place in the marinade about 15 minutes before serving.

When the sweet potato is baked, remove from the oven and leave to cool a little. Once cool enough to handle, thinly slice each half in the skin and arrange on two plates. Scatter over the ceviche and top with cilantro.

Tip

You can try all sorts of fish here—scallops, shrimp, salmon, tuna, and swordfish, for instance—and a teensy-weensy amount of diced avocado adds color, and tastes great, too.

Crab and corn cakes with soy dip

Per serving

184 cals   1.1g fiber

1.6g fat   3.7g salt

0.2g saturated fat

7.3g sugar   **0.8g fat per 100g**

Crab cakes are always a popular choice at my Greyhound pub near Henley-on-Thames. Here, I've given the cakes more texture by adding celery, red bell pepper and corn. Crab is a good source of zinc and iron, and the addition of vegetables will give this dish some fiber, too. A cucumber salad to go with the cakes would add even more fiber.

Serves 4

CRAB CAKES:

spray of vegetable oil

3 scallions, finely chopped

1 stick celery, finely diced

½ red bell pepper, seeded and cut into long thin strips, then diced

2 tablespoons frozen or drained canned corn kernels

11 oz fresh or drained canned white crabmeat

2 egg whites, beaten

1 tablespoon chopped cilantro

1 tablespoon low-sodium soy sauce

⅔ cup (2½ oz) dry white bread crumbs

SOY DIP:

4 tablespoons low-sodium soy sauce

1 scallion, finely chopped

2 teaspoons finely chopped cilantro

1 teaspoon finely chopped mint

1 red bird's eye chile, very finely diced

1 tablespoon mirin (Japanese rice wine (optional)

½ tablespoon honey

For the dip, combine all the ingredients and leave for at least 1 hour to allow the flavors to develop.

For the crab cakes, spray a frying pan with a light coating of oil, then, over medium heat, cook the scallions, celery, and bell pepper for 8–10 minutes, until the vegetables have started to soften. Allow to cool in a bowl.

When the vegetables have cooled, fold in the remaining ingredients and mix well, using your hands. Shape into four large, or eight smaller crab cakes, place in the refrigerator, and ideally leave for a couple of hours to dry out and firm up.

Spray a little oil in a frying pan and cook the crab cakes over medium heat for 2–3 minutes on each side, until golden. Serve with the soy dip.

Tip

Even better, leave the crab cakes covered in the refrigerator overnight before cooking to firm up even more.

Crab, arugula and chili pasta

Per serving
(using canned crab)
301 cals   2.5g fiber
4.7g fat   1.5g salt
0.7g saturated fat
1.2g sugar   **1.5g fat per 100g**

Instant pleasure, so simple and yet really zingy. Fresh crabmeat is preferable but canned is far superior to frozen, if fresh is unavailable. This will take you no time at all. I would rather wait the 10 minutes for dried pasta to cook than shorten the time by using fresh pasta, and as a bonus, crab contains a decent amount of omega-3 fats.

Serves 4

2 large or medium red peppers, finely sliced
2 garlic cloves, crushed to a paste with a
     little sea salt
grated zest and juice of 1 unwaxed lemon
1 tablespoon extra-virgin olive oil
12½ oz fresh or canned white crabmeat
8 oz dried linguine or spaghetti
3 tablespoons roughly chopped parsley
2 handfuls of washed arugula leaves

Add the chile, garlic, lemon zest and juice, and olive oil to the crabmeat and mix to combine. Season to taste.

Heat a large pan of salted water until boiling, then add the pasta and stir until you're sure the pasta will not stick together. Cook until al dente, then drain and return to the pan with a little water still clinging to the pasta. Fold in the parsley and arugula and cook over very low heat until the greens have wilted.

Fold in the crab mixture, cook for another minute, then serve immediately in warm bowls.

Per serving
397 cals   7.4g fiber
5.5g fat   1g salt
0.8g saturated fat
11.8g sugar   **0.9g fat per 100g**

Mediterranean vegetable pasta

When you've got all these exciting flavors, there's no need for meat or fish to come into the equation.

Serves 4

1 tablespoon olive oil
1 red onion, finely chopped
3 garlic cloves, finely chopped
1 oz dry-pack sun-dried tomatoes, chopped
4 canned artichokes, drained and chopped
4 oz roasted red peppers from a jar,
     chopped
1 eggplant, finely diced
1 zucchini, finely diced
14 oz canned cherry tomatoes
11½ oz dried penne
6 basil leaves, shredded

In a large saucepan, heat the olive oil, then add the onion and garlic, and cook slowly for 10 minutes before adding all the remaining vegetables except for the canned tomatoes. Toss to combine and cook for 3 minutes.

Add the canned tomatoes and cook gently for 15 minutes until the sauce thickens, then season well.

Meanwhile, cook the penne in boiling salted water, according to the manufacturer's instructions, or until al dente. Drain in a colander, and, with the water still dripping, add to the sauce. Stir to combine, fold in the basil, and serve immediately with salad and bread.

Vegetable paella

Per serving

449 cals	5.9g fiber
8.5g fat	3.7g salt
2g saturated fat	
8.5g sugar	**1.5g fat per 100g**

Whether you're a vegetarian or not, this dish, rich in earthy flavors, will suit most tastes. Unlike risotto, you don't have to stand over the pan stirring continuously.

Serves 4

30 fl oz vegetable stock
scant cup (7 fl oz) water
1 tablespoon olive oil
1 large onion, finely chopped
3 garlic cloves, finely chopped
2 bay leaves
2 sprigs of thyme
2 dried chiles
1 red bell pepper, seeded and finely
    chopped
pinch of saffron threads
½ teaspoon ground turmeric
2 teaspoons sweet paprika
11½ oz Calasparra or Arborio rice
⅔ cup (4 oz) frozen green peas,
    defrosted
⅔ cup (4 oz) frozen baby fava beans,
    defrosted
1 large zucchini, cut into ¼-inch dice
12 pitted black olives, in brine, drained
2 tablespoons chopped parsley

Heat the stock and water in a pan to boiling.

Meanwhile, in a large frying pan, heat the oil, then cook the onion, garlic, bay leaves, thyme, and chiles gently for 10–12 minutes, until soft, but not brown. Stir in the bell pepper, saffron, turmeric, paprika, and rice until well combined. Cook for 2 minutes.

Add the stock and water, bring to a boil, then reduce the heat, and cook for approximately 18 minutes, until the liquid has evaporated. Stir in the peas, fava beans, zucchini, and olives, cover the pan with a lid, turn off the heat, and leave for 5 minutes.

Season, give it a good stir, then sprinkle with the chopped parsley and serve.

Shrimp tortillas with mango salad

Per serving

422 cals	5.9g fiber
2.3g fat	2g salt
0.3g saturated fat	
18.9g sugar	**0.5g fat per 100g**

These tortillas are quick and easy to make; they're low in fat and high in fiber with the added bonus of two full-on antioxidants—beta-carotene and vitamin C. More importantly, they are delicious.

Serves 4

spray of olive oil
40 raw tiger shrimp, shell off, tail on,
   deveined
2 garlic cloves, finely chopped
1 red pepper, seeded and finely sliced
8 flour tortillas
cilantro sprigs and lime wedges,
   to serve

MANGO SALAD:

½ red onion, finely sliced
3 scallions, finely sliced on
   the diagonal
2 ripe but firm mangoes, peeled,
   pitted and cut into ½-inch dice
1 red chili, seeded and finely diced
8 cherry tomatoes, halved
½ cucumber, peeled, seeded and cut
   into ½-inch dice
6 radishes, finely sliced
1 tablespoon cilantro leaves
1 teaspoon chopped mint
juice of 2 limes and zest of 1 lime
1 tablespoon nam pla (fish sauce)
1 tablespoon honey

For the mango salad, combine all the ingredients in a bowl, check the seasoning, then refrigerate.

Preheat the oven to 325°F.

Spray a griddle pan with oil, set the heat to high, then pan-fry the shrimp for 1 minute on each side. Add the garlic and pepper and cook for another minute, tossing the shrimp from time to time.

Meanwhile, wrap the tortillas in foil and place in the oven to warm through.

To serve, fold the tortillas in four and place two on each plate with 10 shrimp on top, accompanied by the mango salad and some cilantro sprigs and lime wedges. Get your guests to create their own wraps.

Asian chicken burgers

Per serving

383 cals   3.5g fiber

7.3g fat   2g salt

1.4g saturated fat

9.3g sugar   **2g fat per 100g**

We all love burgers, there's no denying it, and that's not such a bad thing. Here, I've reduced the fat by using ground chicken and added a little interest by using Asian ingredients.

Serves 4

1 lb ground chicken (if you can't get it
    use 8 oz each of light and dark meat,
    and grind it yourself in a processor)
2 cups (3 oz) fresh bread crumbs
3 garlic cloves, crushed to a paste
    with a little sea salt
2 Thai red peppers, seeded and
    finely chopped
½ bunch of cilantro, finely chopped
1 tablespoon chopped mint
2 tablespoons sweet chili sauce
1 tablespoon hot chili oil
1 teaspoon ground coriander
4 scallions, finely sliced
2 teaspoons nam pla (fish sauce)
spray of vegetable oil

TO SERVE:

4 onion buns, strips of carrot,
    cucumber shavings, cilantro leaves,
    shaved red onion and tomato slices

Put all the ingredients for the burgers in a clean bowl, and mix well with wet hands. Divide the mixture into four, then shape into patties. Ideally, refrigerate for 1 hour to allow them to firm up.

Spray a large frying pan with vegetable oil and cook the burgers for 4–5 minutes each side over medium heat.

Serve on toasted buns garnished with salad ingredients.

Tip

A good dressing for the salad ingredients would be to mix together 2 teaspoons of superfine sugar, the juice of 2 limes, and 1 tablespoon of nam pla, stirred until the sugar dissolves.

Mussels in a Provençal sauce

Per serving
240 cals   1.5g fiber
7.4g fat   1.9g salt
1g saturated fat
6.2g sugar   **1.1g fat per 100g**

Mussels are probably the sweetest of all the shellfish, and they are definitely the best value. Here, I've put them in a tomato sauce which should be served with crusty bread.

Serves 4

1 tablespoon olive oil
1 onion, finely chopped
3 garlic cloves, finely chopped
2 anchovy fillets, roughly chopped
1 teaspoon chopped thyme leaves
2 bay leaves
¾ cup (6 fl oz) dry white wine
14 oz canned chopped tomatoes
1 teaspoon superfine sugar
2 slices of orange peel
4½ lb cleaned mussels
2 tablespoons chopped Kalamata olives

In a large saucepan, heat the olive oil, then add the onion, garlic, anchovy fillets, thyme, and bay leaves. Cook gently for 10 minutes until the onions have softened.

Add the wine, bring to a boil and cook until most of the liquid has evaporated.

Add the tomatoes, sugar, and orange peel, and cook for 8 minutes before increasing the heat and adding the mussels. Cover with a lid, and cook for 5 minutes, shaking the pan from time to time. Discard any mussels that don't open. Finally fold in the olives, check the seasoning, and serve piping hot with salad and crusty bread.

Spanish shrimp pancakes

Per serving
125 cals   1g fiber
1.7g fat   1.9g salt
0.3g saturated fat
0.7g sugar   **1.2g fat per 100g**

In Spain, you'd get these pancakes made with shell-on shrimp, but I think we'd prefer not to eat head and shells. Either use very small raw shrimp, whole, or larger ones sliced finely. Serve the pancakes with a yogurt dip and salad.

Serves 4

¾ cup (3 oz) all-purpose flour
1 teaspoon baking powder
½ teaspoon salt
½ teaspoon ground black pepper
½ teaspoon sweet paprika
¼ teaspoon chili powder
4 tablespoons chopped parsley
4 scallions, finely chopped
8 oz peeled shrimp (about 1 lb with shells)
1 egg white, beaten to stiff peaks
spray of oil

Sift the flour, baking powder, and salt in a bowl, then add the pepper, paprika, chili powder, parsley. and scallions. Stir to combine, then make a well in the center and gradually add enough water to make a batter the consistency of heavy cream (up to ⅔ cup/5 fl oz) water). Cover with plastic wrap, and set aside for 1 hour.

Fold in the shrimp, then the beaten egg white.

Heat a large, nonstick frying pan, spray with oil, then drop in tablespoons of the batter, spaced apart and allow to spread. Cook over medium heat for about 2 minutes, or until little bubbles appear on the surface. Flip over, and cook for another minute until golden on both sides. Continue until all the pancakes are cooked.

Steak sandwich with onion and mushroom relish

Per serving	
378 cals	5.3g fiber
7.1g fat	1.5g salt
2.3g saturated fat	
19.8g sugar	**2g fat per 100g**

I had to find a way to get a steak sandwich into the recipe list, and, while you don't automatically associate steak with a low-fat diet, I've reduced the meat weight, and upped the vegetables, thereby achieving my aim.

Serves 4

spray of olive oil
4 x 2 oz beef tenderloin steaks,
    trimmed of any fat and beaten thin
8 slices of whole grain bread
handful of baby spinach leaves
1 beefsteak tomato, sliced into 8

ONION AND MUSHROOM RELISH:

1 teaspoon olive oil
3 red onions, finely sliced
1 garlic clove, crushed to a paste
    with a little sea salt
2 tablespoons thyme leaves
½ teaspoon ground black pepper
8 oz button mushrooms, sliced
2 tablespoons brown sugar
2 tablespoons sherry vinegar

To make the onion and mushroom relish, heat the olive oil in a saucepan, add the onion, garlic, thyme, and black pepper, cover with a circle of wet parchment paper, cover with a lid, and cook over very low heat for 45 minutes–1 hour, stirring every 10 minutes or so. The onion will slowly collapse to a caramelized pile.

Discard the parchment paper, then increase the heat, add the mushrooms, and stir to combine. Cook for another 8 minutes, until the mushrooms have released their liquids. Add the brown sugar and vinegar, and cook briefly to combine the flavors, then set aside to keep warm.

Spray the steaks with a little oil, and season with salt and pepper, then cook on a hot griddle pan for 45 seconds–1 minute on both sides.

Toast the bread, then place one slice on each of four plates, top with a loosely arranged pile of spinach, followed by 2 slices of tomato and some relish. Then place the steak on top, followed by a second slice of bread.

Rosemary lamb with beans and penne

Per serving	
516 cals	4.5g fiber
14.9g fat	1.1g salt
5.8g saturated fat	
8.4g sugar	**2.7g fat per 100g**

This is one of those dishes that looks like a bit of a jumble, but the flavors meld—not everything is about looks. It also tastes great at room temperature.

Serves 4

11 oz loin of lamb, trimmed
of visible fat

1 teaspoon olive oil

1 teaspoon ground black pepper

½ teaspoon sea salt

1 teaspoon very finely chopped
rosemary

½ teaspoon ground cumin

1 teaspoon garlic paste

zest and juice of 1 unwaxed lemon

2½ cups (10 oz) dried penne pasta

6 oz extra fine green beans, trimmed
and cut into thirds

1¼ cups (10 fl oz) tomato sauce

14 oz canned green kidney (flageolet)
beans, drained and rinsed

3 tomatoes, seeded and diced

¼ bunch flat-leaf parsley, leaves
picked

Preheat the oven to 350°F.

Place the lamb in a dish and rub with olive oil. Combine the black pepper, salt, rosemary, cumin, garlic paste, and lemon zest. Roll the lamb in this mixture, coating all sides of the meat, then leave for up to 2 hours.

Bring a large pan of salted water to a boil, and cook the penne according to the manufacturer's instructions, keeping the pasta al dente. Drain and keep warm.

Cook the green beans in salted water for 4 minutes, then drain and refresh in cold water.

Heat an ovenproof frying pan, and seal the lamb all over until golden. Do not cook over too high a heat, otherwise you'll scorch the spice coating, rendering it bitter. Place the pan in the oven and cook for 12 minutes, then remove, and allow the lamb to rest in a warm place.

Deglaze the lamb pan with the tomato sauce and lemon juice, and boil for 5 minutes. Add the penne, flageolet beans, and green beans, toss to combine, and heat through. Fold in the tomatoes and parsley leaves and cook until the parsley has wilted. Season well.

Spoon the pasta and beans into four warm bowls, then thinly carve the lamb and arrange on top.

Poached pollock with fennel sauce

Per serving
402 cals   5.6g fiber
6.8g fat   0.9g salt
1.8g saturated fat
19.2g sugar   **1g fat per 100g**

Pollock is a sustainable fish, but personally I don't think it's a fish that stands alone; it needs a sauce. So this sauce encompasses the flavor of the fennel that goes well with the fish, but it also includes several other vegetables.

Serves 4

3 scant cups (23 fl oz) skim milk

1 bay leaf

pinch of grated nutmeg

2 carrots, peeled and cut into
 ½-inch dice

1 head of fennel, outside layer
 removed, then cut into ½-inch dice

8 new potatoes, peeled or not,
 cut into ½-inch dice

1 onion, finely sliced

4 x 6 oz fillets of pollock

3 tablespoons low-fat spread

⅓ cup flour

⅔ cup (4 oz) frozen green peas,
 defrosted

2 tomatoes, seeded and diced

2 teaspoons chopped dill

Place the milk in a saucepan with the bay leaf, nutmeg, carrots, fennel, new potatoes, and onion. Bring to a boil, and simmer for 15–20 minutes to cook the vegetables.

Place the pollock in the milk and poach for 5 minutes, then remove and keep warm. Strain the milk, retaining both the milk and vegetables separately, but discarding the bay leaf. Keep the milk hot.

Place the low-fat spread in a nonstick pan with the cooked vegetables. When the spread has melted, and is bubbling, add the flour and stir to combine. Gradually add the cooked milk, stirring constantly. You will not need all the milk, you're looking for a sauce the thickness of heavy cream. But as it cooks, the sauce will thicken, so keep adding the milk until the sauce no longer tastes floury, probably about 15 minutes. Season well. Finally, fold in the peas, tomatoes, and dill.

Place the pollock in a suitable baking dish, then pour over the hot sauce, and place under the broiler until the sauce and fish bubble gently. Serve piping hot.

Tip

The trick to a good béchamel-style sauce is to cook the roux (flour and fat) for a few minutes, then cook the sauce for long enough to eliminate that floury taste.

Color-coordinated sweet potato

Per serving
225 cals
1.2g fat
0.3g saturated fat
16.5g sugar

5.9g fiber
0.3g salt

0.4g fat per 100g

Why don't we eat more sweet potatoes? They're yummy, with a natural sweetness and great color. Treat them exactly as you would normal potatoes, though they cook a little quicker and they've got a better GI rating. With these baked potatoes, all you need is a salad.

Serves 4

4 medium sweet potatoes (approx. 6½ oz each), washed
½ red onion, sliced
2 scallions, finely sliced
1 tablespoon roughly chopped cilantro
¼ teaspoon ground cumin
½ teaspoon Tabasco
2 tablespoons fat-free Greek yogurt
1 tablespoon sweet chili sauce
juice of 1 lime
½ red bell pepper, finely diced
½ cup (4½ oz) corn kernels, drained
⅓ cup (2 oz) frozen green peas, defrosted
3 oz canned chunk light tuna in spring water, drained

Preheat the oven to 400°F.

Place the sweet potatoes on a rack set over a baking sheet, and cook for approximately 40 minutes, or until tender when pierced with a knife.

Meanwhile, combine the remaining ingredients in a bowl and leave for the flavors to develop while the potatoes are cooking. Season.

Cut a deep cross in each of the sweet potatoes and prise open. Spoon a quarter of the mixture into each one.

Tip

Feel free to substitute shrimp, canned crab, or canned salmon for the tuna for a change, and the mixture also works well with shredded, cooked turkey or chicken.

A warm salad of pumpkin, mint, and chile

Per serving

63 cals   3g fiber
0.9g fat   1.5g salt
0.3g saturated fat
9g sugar   **0.3g fat per 100g**

This is such a tasty vegetarian dish, and nowadays I eat more and more of this style of food, reducing my meat intake, and putting loads of flavor into delicious vegetables. Think of the pumpkin as an orange zucchini, requiring very little cooking. In fact, the salad works very well with zucchini or butternut squash instead of the pumpkin, and with arugula added in place of the spinach.

Serves 4

2½ lb pumpkin, peeled, seeded and
    thinly sliced in manageable pieces
3 garlic cloves, thinly sliced
3 Thai bird's eye chiles, thinly sliced
spray of vegetable oil
4 oz snow peas, trimmed and
    thinly sliced
4 scallions, thinly sliced on
    the diagonal
¼ cup vegetable stock
3 tablespoons low-sodium
    soy sauce
1-inch piece of fresh ginger, peeled
    and cut into julienne (small strips)
2 teaspoons honey
12 mint leaves
2 handfuls of baby spinach, washed

Put the pumpkin, garlic, and chile in a bowl and spray with oil. Toss to combine, then season with salt and pepper.

Heat a large saucepan, add the pumpkin mixture, then cover with a lid and cook for 6 minutes, shaking the pan from time to time.

Remove the lid, add the snow peas, scallions, vegetable stock, soy sauce, and ginger, and cook over medium heat for 3 minutes. Finally, add the honey, mint, and spinach and stir to combine. Cook until the spinach starts to wilt, about 1 minute.

Serve hot or at room temperature.

Flash-fried rice

Per serving

388 cals	3.4g fiber
8.8g fat	1.8g salt
2.3g saturated fat	
12.4g sugar	**2.4g fat per 100g**

I'm a bit of a fan of fried rice. It's just that the word "fried" doesn't instill confidence for those on a low-fat diet. However, I've discovered a different method that produces a similar effect, but doesn't need very much fat.

Serves 4

2 cups (1 lb) instant microwavable long-grain rice, cooked (see Tip)

spray of oil

4 scallions, finely sliced

2 long green peppers, finely sliced

1 red bell pepper, seeded and cut into thin strips

4 oz extra fine green beans, trimmed and cut into 1-inch pieces

⅓ cup (2 oz) frozen green peas, defrosted

¼ winter (Savoy) cabbage, shredded and washed

11½ oz skinless cooked chicken, diced

1 tablespoon dark brown sugar

½ chicken stock cube, crumbled

2 tablespoons low-sodium soy sauce

2 tablespoons sweet chili sauce

½ bunch of roughly chopped cilantro

Preheat the oven to 400°F.

Line a shallow baking pan with nonstick parchment paper. Tip the rice onto the paper, breaking up any lumps, and spray the surface with oil. Place in the oven, and cook for 12 minutes—it should be crisp on the surface. Season, and set aside to keep warm.

Meanwhile, spray a wok (ideally nonstick) with a good coating of oil and, over high heat, fry the scallions, chiles, bell pepper, and beans for 2 minutes, stirring continuously.

Add the peas, cabbage, and chicken, and fry to give a little color, and to wilt the cabbage, about 3 minutes.

Sprinkle over the sugar and stock cube, then add the rice, breaking up any lumps. Stir-fry for 2 minutes, then add the remaining ingredients. Cook for 1 minute, then serve very hot.

Tip

I know it's lazy, but I'm a supporter of quick-cook rice. If you feel you want to cook your own from scratch, feel free, but make sure that you cool it quickly after cooking, and make sure that it is very dry, and that the grains are separate—use paper towels, if necessary.

Tagliatelle with cumin-roasted cherry tomatoes

Per serving

317 cals	4.8g fiber
3.1g fat	0.3g salt
0.5g saturated fat	
4.9g sugar	**0.8g fat per 100g**

A little pre-planning is required for this pasta dish, but I think it's worth the effort. Sacrifice some time in the name of simplicity, because the roasting process really intensifies the tomato flavor and increases the fiber content.

Serves 4

1 lb cherry tomatoes, halved
spray of olive oil
3 garlic cloves, very finely chopped
¼ teaspoon crushed red pepper flakes
2 teaspoons cumin seeds
1 teaspoon fennel seeds
12 oz dried tagliatelle
6 basil leaves, torn
handful of baby spinach leaves

Preheat the oven to 275°F.

Arrange the cherry tomatoes, cut-side up, on a baking pan lined with parchment paper. Spray the tomatoes with a mist of olive oil, then scatter with the chopped garlic and chili flakes and sprinkle with the seeds. Place in the preheated oven for about 1 hour, or until the tomatoes have slightly shriveled, but not become too brown.

Toward the halfway stage of the tomatoes cooking, start thinking about the pasta by bringing a large pan of salted water to a boil. Add the pasta 10 minutes before the tomatoes are ready, stir for a couple of minutes, then cook until al dente—which is about 1 minute less than the manufacturer recommends.

Remove the tomatoes from the oven and tip them, with any juices, into a frying pan. Drain the pasta using a pasta ladle, then ladle onto the tomatoes with a little of the cooking water. Carefully place the basil and spinach on top of the pasta, and continue to toss or turn over the pasta until the spinach has wilted. You're bound to lose a few leaves to the stove top, so you may prefer to add the spinach little by little.

Season to taste and serve immediately.

Tip

You may be tempted to use sun-dried tomatoes in olive oil. *Don't!* It's cheating; they don't taste as good, and in any case they're saturated in olive oil.

Per serving

150 cals	4.7g fiber
3g fat	1.3g salt
0.6g saturated fat	
10.2g sugar	**0.7g fat per 100g**

A simple vegetable curry

You must not feel daunted by the idea of making curry at home—it's just a case of having a few spices in your cupboard. This curry can be easily adapted to suit different tastes. If you choose different vegetables, just make sure you add them at the right time; if using more root vegetables, for example, add them at the same time as the potatoes.

Serves 8

1 tablespoon vegetable oil

1 onion, roughly chopped

1 teaspoon grated fresh ginger

4 garlic cloves, crushed to a paste
  with a little sea salt

½ teaspoon chili powder

1 teaspoon ground cumin

1 teaspoon ground coriander

½ teaspoon ground fennel

3 cardamom pods, lightly crushed

½ teaspoon ground black pepper

1 teaspoon ground turmeric

8 new potatoes, halved

2½ cups (20 fl oz) vegetable stock

½ butternut squash, peeled, seeded
  and cut into 1-inch dice

½ cauliflower, broken into florets

2 zucchini, cut into 1-inch rounds

3 tomatoes, roughly chopped

1 teaspoon garam masala

½ cup (3 oz) frozen green peas,
  defrosted

2 medium-heat green peppers,
  seeded and sliced

2 handfuls of baby spinach leaves

4 tablespoons fat-free Greek yogurt

Heat the oil in a large saucepan, then cook the onion, ginger, and garlic over low heat for 10–12 minutes until the onion starts to soften. Add the spices, toss to combine, and cook for 1 minute.

Add the halved potatoes and cook until they start to stick slightly, then pour in the stock, bring to a boil and cook for 5 minutes. Add the butternut squash, cauliflower, and zucchini, and cook for 6 minutes.

Fold in the tomatoes, garam masala, peas, chiles, and spinach, stir to combine and cook for 3 minutes. Check the seasoning, and serve with rice and a dollop of yogurt.

Spiced chicken livers

Per serving
250 cals
5.9g fat
0.9g saturated fat
9.5g sugar

4.7g fiber
1g salt

1.5g fat per 100g

Offal, apart from calf's liver, generally offers exceptional value, and chicken livers are also very nutritious. If you love your liver, like me, you'll really enjoy this quick, good-value dish. Serve with crusty bread.

Serves 4

1 lb chicken livers, trimmed
   and cubed
4 tablespoons fat-free Greek yogurt
½ teaspoon ground cumin
½ teaspoon ground coriander
½ teaspoon ground fennel
1 teaspoon ground turmeric
4 garlic cloves, mashed to a paste
   with a little sea salt
2 onions, 1 roughly chopped,
   1 finely sliced
1 teaspoon grated fresh ginger
1 medium-heat chili, seeded
   and roughly chopped
3 tablespoon tikka paste
½ bunch of cilantro, roughly chopped
spray of vegetable oil
14 oz canned chopped tomatoes
1 teaspoon rose harissa
14 oz canned cannellini beans, rinsed
   and drained

Combine the chicken livers with the yogurt, cumin, coriander, fennel, turmeric, and half the garlic, and leave to marinate while you cook the sauce.

Put the remaining garlic in a food processor with the roughly chopped onion, ginger, chili, tikka paste, and cilantro and blend to a smooth purée. Set aside.

Spray a saucepan with the vegetable oil, add the onion slices and cook over medium heat for 5 minutes to soften them. Add the puréed onion paste, along with the chopped tomatoes, and bring to a boil. Reduce the heat and simmer for 15 minutes.

Meanwhile, scrape the yogurt off the livers, and add this to the pan. Stir to combine.

Heat a frying pan with oil and, over a fierce heat, fry the chicken livers for 1 minute each side. Transfer to the tomato sauce with the harissa and beans. Warm through and season.

Sea bass carpaccio with shaved vegetables

Per serving
114 cals   1.7g fiber
3.7g fat   0.2g salt
0.6g saturated fat
3.4g sugar   **1.8g fat per 100g**

I do like raw fish, but it obviously has to be incredibly fresh. This recipe "cooks" the sea bass by marination. Vegetable shavings look really cute on the plate, and the crunch is in contrast to the soft texture of the sea bass.

Serves 4

1 small fennel bulb, outside layer removed, then cut into paper-thin slivers

1 carrot, peeled and thinly shaved using a peeler

½ cucumber, peeled and shaved using a peeler (discard seeds)

4 radishes, very thinly sliced

1 teaspoon chopped mint

1 teaspoon chopped dill

1 teaspoon superfine sugar

¼ teaspoon sea salt

¼ teaspoon ground white pepper

juice of 1 lemon

2 teaspoons extra-virgin olive oil

12 oz sea bass fillets

In a bowl, combine the fennel, carrot, cucumber, and radishes. Toss to combine.

In a separate bowl, combine the mint, dill, sugar, salt, pepper, and lemon juice. Stir to combine then add the olive oil.

Slice the sea bass paper thin with a sharp knife (you should be able to see the knife through the sea bass) and arrange on four cold plates.

Scatter the vegetable ribbons over the sea bass, then drizzle the herb dressing over the vegetables. Leave for 20 minutes before serving.

Tip

This recipe works well with salmon, although the fat content will be higher, or you could try thinly sliced scallops, swordfish, or raw oysters.

Spaghetti with red peppers and shellfish

Per serving
385 cal   4.1g fiber
4.3g fat   1.3g salt
0.7g saturated fat
3.9g sugar   **1g fat per 100g**

I usually avoid cooked seafood at the supermarket, but occasionally, when pushed for time, I'll use it—and it's not bad.

Serves 4

2 roasted red peppers from a jar, well drained and roughly chopped

2 medium-hot red peppers, seeded and roughly chopped

3 garlic cloves, roughly chopped

2 scallions, roughly chopped

2 tablespoons white wine vinegar

1 tablespoon tomato paste

12 basil leaves

12 oz dried spaghetti

12 oz mixed cooked shellfish (shrimp, mussels, squid, and crab)

Place the peppers, chiles, garlic, scallions, vinegar, tomato paste, and basil in a blender and purée until almost smooth. Season and set aside.

Meanwhile, heat a deep saucepan of salted water until boiling. Cook the spaghetti for 1 minute less than the manufacturer's instructions.

While the spaghetti is cooking, gently heat the red pepper sauce, then add the seafood and warm through. Using a pasta ladle, drain the spaghetti and, with water still clinging to it, add to the seafood sauce. Toss well and serve immediately.

Tip

Don't feel like shellfish? Cut some white fish fillets into 1-inch cubes and cook these through in the sauce before adding the pasta.

Flash-fried venison with a herb salad

Per serving

122 cals   2g fiber

4.5g fat   2.9g salt

1.2g saturated fat

5g sugar   **1.6g fat per 100g**

Venison is a meat that's reasonably low in fat, but it is also tender and full of flavor. Here, I've placed it in an unusual Asian setting, showing the versatility of the game. The herb salad is deliciously refreshing.

Serves 4

2 tablespoons nam pla (fish sauce)

2 stalks of lemongrass, outside layer removed and roughly chopped

1 red pepper, seeded and roughly chopped

3 scallions, roughly chopped

1 teaspoon vegetable oil

2 garlic cloves, roughly chopped

2 teaspoons low-sodium soy sauce

8 mint leaves

8 oz venison loin, thinly sliced

SALAD:

1 Baby Gem lettuce, leaves separated

1 bunch of watercress, tough stems removed

1 small bunch of mint, leaves only

1 small bunch of cilantro, leaves and tender stems only

1 small bunch of dill, tougher stems removed

3 scallions, cut into julienne

4 radishes, quartered

8 cherry tomatoes, halved

½ cucumber, peeled, seeded and cut into ½-inch pieces

½ teaspoon garlic purée

1 shallot, peeled and grated

1 tablespoon nam pla (fish sauce)

½ teaspoon superfine sugar

1 hard-boiled egg, yolk only

1 tablespoon lime juice

In a food processor, blend the fish sauce, lemongrass, pepper, scallions, oil, garlic, soy sauce, and mint leaves until fairly smooth. Add the venison slices to the marinade, and leave for at least 2 hours, ideally overnight.

Just before cooking the venison, combine the lettuce, watercress, mint, cilantro, dill, scallions, radishes, cherry tomatoes, and cucumber and arrange in a bowl.

Whisk together the garlic purée, grated shallot, fish sauce, sugar, egg yolk, and lime juice and pour over the salad, tossing to combine.

Place a wok over high heat and quickly pan-fry the venison slices for 1–3 minutes, depending on how thickly you've cut the venison. It should be brown on the outside and pink on the inside.

Arrange the pan-fried venison over the salad just before serving.

Main courses

Roast sea bass on Mediterranean vegetables

Per serving	
248 cals	2.4g fiber
8.2g fat	0.5g salt
1.3g saturated fat	
6.3g sugar	**2.1g fat per 100g**

Loads of flavor, loads of vitamins and minerals, with sea bass also providing useful pantothenic acid, a B vitamin that helps to keep the nervous system healthy, and other B vitamins, but forget all that, it's a delicious dinner party dish.

Serves 4

2 zucchini cut in 1-inch chunks
4 scallions, cut in half
4 garlic cloves peeled
1 red bell pepper, stalk and seeds
    removed, cut in 1-inch squares
16 cherry tomatoes, halved
3 sprigs thyme, leaves stripped
1 sprig rosemary, leaves stripped
1 tablespoon extra-virgin olive oil
spray of olive oil
4 x 6 oz fillets of sea bass
6 basil leaves, torn
1 tablespoon balsamic vinegar

Preheat the oven to 425°F.

Place the first seven ingredients in a bowl and toss with the extra-virgin olive oil, salt and pepper. Tip everything into a baking pan and place in the oven for 20 minutes.

Spray a nonstick frying pan with olive oil, heat to very hot, season the sea bass fillets, and place them skin-side down in the pan. Sea bass tends to curl up, so push the fillets flat with a fish slice. Cook them for 2 minutes to brown the skin.

Remove the roast vegetables from the oven, and place the sea bass fillets skin-side up on top of the vegetables. Return to the oven for 10 minutes. Lift the fish onto four warm plates, then toss the vegetables with the basil leaves and the balsamic vinegar. Serve immediately with the fish.

Tip

These vegetables make a very good salad served at room temperature.

Steamed fish in lettuce and ginger

Per serving

236 cals	2.5g fiber
5.9g fat	1.9g salt
1g saturated fat	
5.8g sugar	**1.9g fat per 100g**

Everyone who diets, and let's face it—that seems to be most of us, needs a steamer; it doesn't need to be sophisticated, it could be just a bamboo basket set over a wok. Incidentally, when we think of steaming, we must not think of hospital food—this dish has loads of flavor.

Serves 4

8 romaine lettuce leaves (the outer ones)

4 x 6 oz sea bass or other white fish fillets

4-inch piece of fresh ginger, peeled and cut into very thin strips

4 scallions, cut into thin strips

½ teaspoon garlic paste

2 teaspoons rice vinegar

1 teaspoon sesame oil

1 teaspoon honey

4 tablespoons low-sodium soy sauce

1 medium-hot red chili, seeded and thinly sliced

⅔ cup (4 oz) frozen green peas, defrosted

8 spears of asparagus, trimmed and lower section peeled

Half fill a wok with water and bring to a boil. Blanch the lettuce leaves for 30 seconds until they wilt. Lift out and refresh in cold water, then drain and pat dry with paper towels. (Reserve the boiling water for steaming later.)

Cut out the thickest part of the central rib of each lettuce leaf and lay four piles of two slightly overlapping leaves on your work surface. Place the sea bass fillets, skin-side down, on the four lettuce squares. Scatter with the ginger and scallion strips.

Whisk together the garlic, vinegar, sesame oil, honey, and soy sauce in a bowl.

Scatter a few peas over the fish, together with two spears of asparagus. Working on one pile at a time, drizzle a little of the soy mixture over the fish, then scatter over the chili and enclose with the lettuce. Repeat with the other fish and place on a plate that will fit inside a bamboo steamer.

Place the bamboo steamer over a wok of boiling water, cover with a lid and steam for 8–10 minutes.

Serve with rice and a little more of the marinade.

Monkfish and prosciutto skewers with thyme tomatoes

Per serving
220 cals   1.1g fiber
5g fat   1.8g salt
1.4g saturated fat
3.1g sugar   **1.8g fat per 100g**

Monkfish is a wonderfully meaty fish, which has the cooking qualities of meat, and cooks well on the barbecue or griddle pan. It also contains a good quantity of the vitamin B group as well as trace minerals.

Serves 4

grated zest of 1 unwaxed lemon

1 sprig of rosemary, leaves stripped and finely chopped

¼ teaspoon ground black pepper

1½ lb monkfish fillet, skin and cartilege removed, cut into 12 x 1-inch pieces

6 slices prosciutto (Parma or Serrano ham), fat removed and each cut in 2 lengthwise

2 garlic cloves, crushed to a paste with a little sea salt

2 sprigs of thyme, leaves stripped

2 teaspoons capers, drained, rinsed and finely chopped

4 beefsteak tomatoes, each cut into 3 horizontally

spray of olive oil

Preheat the oven to 300°F.

On a flat dish combine the lemon zest, rosemary, and black pepper then roll the monkfish pieces in the mix. Lay the strips of prosciutto lengthwise on your work surface. Place a piece of fish at one end of each slice and roll up. Thread two rolls on each skewer (if using wooden skewers, pre-soak them in cold water for an hour), then set aside until you are ready to cook.

Meanwhile, mash together the garlic, thyme, and capers. Spray each slice of tomato with olive oil, then spread with a little of the garlicky paste and sprinkle with black pepper. Cook for 1 hour, then increase the temperature to 425°F, and cook for another 10 minutes.

Heat a griddle pan, large frying pan or barbecue. Spray the skewers with a light coating of oil, and cook them for 6–7 minutes over medium heat, turning once.

Place a fish roll on each slice of tomato, and serve three to a plate, accompanied by a green salad.

Tip

While the tomatoes are slow-cooking, the fish will marinate nicely with the lemon and rosemary.

Poached salmon in a herb and tomato broth

Per serving

222 cals   1.3g fiber

8.8g fat   2.3g salt

4.4g saturated fat

6.4g sugar   **2.4g fat per 100g**

This is a delicate way to cook fish that is also extremely healthy. The broth has flavors reminiscent of salsa verde, but without so much oil. Serve with new potatoes.

Serves 4

2 teaspoons olive oil

1 red onion, finely diced

1 garlic clove, finely chopped

2 sprigs of thyme, leaves stripped

½ teaspoon toasted fennel seeds

2 anchovy fillets, rinsed, drained
  and chopped

2 teaspoons Lilliput (baby) capers

2 gherkins, finely chopped

2 teaspoons Worcestershire sauce

1²/₃ cups (13 fl oz) dashi, fish, or vegetable
  stock

4 x 6 oz fillets of salmon

3 tomatoes, seeded and diced

3 tablespoons finely chopped parsley

In a large saucepan, over medium heat, cook the onion with the olive oil for 6–8 minutes, then add the garlic, thyme, fennel seeds, and anchovies and cook gently for another 3 minutes.

Add the capers, gherkins, Worcestershire sauce, and stock, and bring to a boil. Cook for 5 minutes, then add the fish fillets, cook for 5 minutes more, and fold in the tomatoes and parsley. Season and serve in bowls.

Tip

This dish also works well with monkfish, red snapper, sea bass, and halibut.

A butter bean stew

Per serving

210 cals   7.4g fiber

3.1g fat   0.4g salt

0.8g saturated fat

12.3g sugar   **0.8g fat per 100g**

Serves 4

2 teaspoons olive oil

2 onions, roughly chopped

6 garlic cloves, roughly chopped

2 sticks of celery, thinly sliced

1 carrot, thinly sliced

1 teaspoon fennel seeds

¼ teaspoon ground cinnamon

1 teaspoon dried oregano

1 teaspoon superfine sugar

14 oz canned chopped tomatoes

2 teaspoons tomato paste

28 oz canned lima beans, drained
  and rinsed

½ cup (4 oz) low-fat cottage cheese

2 teaspoons chopped fresh oregano

Heat the olive oil in a saucepan, then add the onions and cook for 10 minutes over medium heat so as to soften, but not brown them. Add the garlic, celery, carrot, and fennel seeds, and cook over medium heat for another 3 minutes.

Add the cinnamon, oregano, sugar, canned tomatoes, and tomato paste and stir to combine. Bring to a boil, then reduce the heat and simmer for 25 minutes.

Add the beans and cook for another 15 minutes. Spoon into four warm bowls, then crumble over the cottage cheese and fresh oregano.

Tip

This stew works well with all sorts of canned beans, excluding the baked variety.

Swordfish with citrus notes

Per serving

330 cals   3.3g fiber

11.9g fat   1.5g salt

2.4g saturated fat

3.1g sugar   **3g fat per 100g**

Swordfish, like tuna and marlin, are very meaty fish that don't benefit from being overcooked. The topping works well with the citrus flavors cutting through the richness of the fish.

Serves 4

1 lb new potatoes

11 oz broccoli florets

4 x 6 oz swordfish steaks

spray of olive oil

CITRUS SALSA:

1 tablespoon extra-virgin olive oil

juice and grated zest of 1 unwaxed lemon

juice and grated zest of ½ navel orange

1 mild long red chili, seeded and
   finely diced

2 scallions, finely chopped

1 garlic clove, finely chopped

1½ tablespoons Lilliput (baby) capers,
   rinsed and drained

8 pitted Kalamata olives in brine, rinsed
   and finely chopped

1 tablespoon chopped mint

2 teaspoons snipped chives

Combine the salsa ingredients in a bowl, and leave the flavors to develop for 20 minutes. Season to taste.

Meanwhile, in a pan of boiling water, cook the new potatoes for 12–15 minutes until nearly tender, then add the broccoli and cook for another 4 minutes. Carefully drain and season. Keep warm.

Heat a griddle pan or large frying pan until almost smoking. Season the swordfish with salt and pepper, and spray a fine mist of olive oil over the surface of the fish. Cook over a fierce heat for 1 minute on each side. Turn off the heat and allow the steaks to sit for 3 minutes in the residual heat.

Serve with the broccoli and new potatoes, with the citrus salsa scattered over the fish.

Roast butternut squash with a Chinese influence

Per serving

162 cal	5.7g fiber
0.5g fat	3.9g salt
0.1g saturated fat	
22g sugar	**0.1g fat per 100**

One of my favorite vegetables of all time. I use it in all sorts of guises, but I particularly like it roasted, as here, where the Chinese flavors give it a lovely richness. Roasting doesn't have to mean using oil—this dish is completely free from added fat, but still looks and tastes amazing.

Serves 4

3 small red onions, cut in rough
  chunks or wedges
12 garlic cloves, left whole and peeled
½ cup (4 fl oz) vegetable stock
1 large butternut squash, peeled,
  seeded and cut into 1½-inch chunks
3 tablespoons low-sodium soy sauce
3 tablespoons Chinese oyster sauce
1 tablespoon sweet chili sauce
1 tablespoon lime juice
1 tablespoon honey
2 tablespoons torn basil leaves,
  ideally Thai
2 tablespoons cilantro leaves

TO SERVE:

red chili slices
lime wedges
brown rice

Preheat the oven to 375°F.

Toss the onions, garlic, vegetable stock, and butternut squash together and place in a deep roasting pan. Place the pan in the oven, and roast for 40–50 minutes, until the butternut squash is fork tender.

Meanwhile, combine the soy sauce, oyster sauce, chili sauce, lime juice, and honey in a bowl. Pour the mixture over the squash, stir to combine and return to the oven for 5 minutes.

Spoon into a serving dish, sprinkle with the herbs and sliced chiles, and squeeze the lime over the top. Serve as a meal with brown rice, or as an accompaniment to fish or chicken.

Tip

This recipe will work with all varieties of the squash and pumpkin family.

Chili non carne

Per serving (based on 6 portions)

301 cals	8.1g fiber
5g fat	2.4g salt
0.8g saturated fat	
13.2g sugar	**1.1g fat per 100g**

Everyone loves chili, so there's no reason why low-fat vegetarians shouldn't get involved in the chili process. You're looking for all the flavors without the meat, thereby achieving your low-fat targets at the same time. Feel free to use different vegetables as long as you're sticking to the flavor base. This is a real kitchen cupboard recipe.

Serves 4–6

1 cup (5½ oz) quinoa or bulgur
   (cracked) wheat
9 fl oz very hot water
2 teaspoons olive oil
1 onion, roughly chopped
3 garlic cloves, crushed to a paste
   with a little sea salt
2 green peppers, seeded and finely
   chopped
1 stick celery, finely chopped
1 bay leaf
1 teaspoon dried oregano
1 teaspoon ground cumin
1 teaspoon ground coriander
1 teaspoon sweet paprika
½ teaspoon cayenne pepper
½ teaspoon ground fennel
½ teaspoon ground cinnamon
28 oz canned chopped tomatoes
scant 2 cups (15 fl oz) vegetable stock
14 oz canned red kidney beans, drained
   and rinsed
14 oz canned cannellini beans, drained
   and rinsed
14 oz canned chickpeas, drained
   and rinsed
11½ oz canned corn kernels, drained
1 teaspoon unsweetened cocoa
   powder
2 tablespoons chopped cilantro leaves

Put the quinoa in a bowl, pour over the hot water, and allow to soak for 12 minutes.

In a large saucepan, heat the olive oil and gently cook the onion for 8–10 minutes until softened, but not colored. Add the garlic, chiles, and celery, and cook for another 2 minutes. Fold in the herbs and spices, and stir to combine.

Add the canned tomatoes, stock, and quinoa, and stir. Bring to a boil over medium heat, reduce the heat, and cook gently for 20 minutes. Add all of the canned vegetables, and cook gently for 15 minutes. Fold in the cocoa powder and cilantro and season to taste.

Serve piping hot with fat-free Greek yogurt, some diced raw tomatoes and red onion, and some tortilla chips.

Mixed vegetable burger

Per serving

358 cals	4g fiber
4.4g fat	1.1g salt
1.3g saturated fat	
10g sugar	**1.3g fat per 100g**

As a vegetarian you still want to enjoy some frivolous food, but why not make the burger yourself rather than buy something that appears to have been manufactured by a scientist? Whether you're a vegetarian or not, these are delicious, and they are a great source of fiber, folate, potassium, and antioxidants.

Serves 4

14 oz canned green kidney (flageolet) beans or cannellini beans, drained and rinsed

spray of olive oil

1 onion, finely chopped

3 garlic cloves, mashed to a paste with a little sea salt

2 green peppers, seeded and finely chopped

1 teaspoon ground cumin

½ teaspoon ground coriander

½ teaspoon ground fennel

1 zucchini, grated

½ red bell pepper, seeded and cut into ½-inch dice

2 scallions, finely sliced

2 cups (3 oz) soft fresh bread crumbs

1 tablespoon whole wheat flour

4 tablespoons ricotta cheese

TO SERVE:

4 pita breads, toasted

handful of salad leaves or arugula

1 beefsteak tomato, cut into 4 slices

4 tablespoons fat-free Greek yogurt (optional)

In a large bowl, mash the beans with a fork or potato masher, retaining a little texture.

Spray a frying pan with oil, and cook the onion over medium heat for 6–8 minutes until softened, but not colored. Add the garlic paste, chiles, and spices, and cook for another 3 minutes, stirring regularly. Allow to cool.

Add the zucchini, bell pepper, scallions, bread crumbs, and flour to the onions, and use your hands to combine the mixture, squeezing to compress the ingredients together. Divide the mixture into four balls.

Take one ball in your hands and flatten to create a burger shape. Make an indent in the center with your thumb, and place a quarter of the ricotta in the hole, bringing the mixture up to enclose the cheese. Repeat with the other three burgers. Ideally refrigerate for a couple of hours to firm up the burgers.

Using a frying pan sprayed with oil, cook the burgers for 3–4 minutes on each side or until golden brown. Once browned, you could finish them in the oven (preheated to 350°F) if you wish.

Cut the pita in half horizontally, fill with the salad and tomato slices, followed by the burger and, if desired, a dollop of yogurt.

Veal scallopini with prosciutto and basil

Per serving

272 cals   2.1g fiber
9g fat   1.3g salt
2.2g saturated fat
6.6g sugar   **2.5g fat per 100g**

This dish, based loosely on veal saltimbocca, is a simple, no-hassle dinner party-style dish. Some of you, like me, will be concerned about the welfare of veal calves, but in the US we can now buy free range veal, which is reared in a humane way; its flesh is not as white as that of traditional veal, but the flavor is better. Alternatively, you could substitute pork tenderloin or pounded chicken breast, but veal is naturally a low-fat meat.

Serves 4

4 x 4 oz free range veal scallopini,
    pounded thin
8 basil leaves
4 slices of prosciutto (Parma or
    Serrano ham), fat removed
1 tablespoon olive oil
1 garlic clove, lightly crushed
1 whole dried red pepper
seasoned flour, for coating
½ cup (4 fl oz) dry white wine

FOR THE SALAD:

8 tomatoes on the vine, quartered
½ red onion, finely sliced
8 basil leaves, torn
2 teaspoons extra-virgin olive oil
1 tablespoon balsamic vinegar

Lay the veal scallopini on your work surface, top each with two basil leaves, season, then top with the prosciutto, pressing down to create a seal.

Heat the oil in a large frying pan with the garlic and chili, and cook until the garlic is golden, and the chili has darkened, turning both from time to time; the oil should not be too hot; the idea being to release the flavor of the garlic and chili rather than burn them. Discard the solids.

Dust the veal on both sides with seasoned flour, then place it, prosciutto-side down, into the flavored oil. Cook for 2 minutes over medium heat, then turn over and cook for another 2 minutes. Remove and set aside to keep warm.

Meanwhile, for the salad, combine all the ingredients and season to taste.

Pour the wine into the frying pan and stir well to loosen any meat residue from the bottom of the pan. Season, then pour over the veal and serve immediately.

Tip

Some like to secure the ham to the veal with toothpicks, but this is not necessary, if you are careful when you turn the scallops over. Always cook the ham side of the veal first.

Asian chicken, rice, and peas

Per serving

387 cals   3.8g fiber

8.9g fat   2.9g salt

1.7g saturated fat

14.1g sugar   **1.8g fat per 100g**

I'm a fan of the chicken and rice you see all over Singapore, which inspired this little number; it's simple, very tasty, and good value.

Serves 4

1 tablespoon canola or vegetable oil

2 large onions, thinly sliced

1 teaspoon chopped garlic

1 teaspoon fresh grated ginger

1 tablespoon dashi stock powder

1¼ cups (10 fl oz) boiling water

2 tablespoons Japanese soy sauce

3 fl oz mirin (Japanese rice wine)

1 tablespoon honey

2 large chicken breasts, thinly sliced

6 oz sugar snap peas, trimmed

6 shiitake mushrooms, stems removed and quartered

2 free-range eggs, lightly beaten

3 cups (11 oz) instant brown rice

4 scallions, thinly sliced on the diagonal

2 long green peppers, seeded and thinly sliced

Heat the oil in a large saucepan and cook the onions gently for 15 minutes. Increase the temperature, add the garlic and ginger, and cook for another 5 minutes to lightly brown the onions.

Whisk the dashi powder into the boiling water, then add the soy sauce, mirin, and honey, and simmer for 5 minutes before adding the onion mixture.

Add the chicken, sugar snap peas, and mushrooms, and cook for 5 minutes with the liquid boiling. Pour in the beaten eggs in a steady stream, stirring the liquid as you do to create egg strands.

Cook the rice either in the microwave, or according to the instructions on the packet. Spoon into four bowls, then top with the chicken and egg broth. Garnish with the scallions and chiles.

Tip

Many supermarkets sell dashi stock nowadays, especially Asian markets, but if you can't find it just substitute chicken stock.

Braised cod with spices and tomatoes

Per serving

282 cals   3.2g fiber

4.7g fat   0.9g salt

0.6g saturated fat

10.2g sugar   **1g fat per 100g**

This is a delicious way to serve white fish, and also makes an excellent dinner-party dish. By now we all know how good cooked tomatoes are for us, so with the added benefits of fish, you can eat without guilt. Serve with brown rice.

Serves 4

½ cup (2 oz) seasoned flour

4 x 6 oz cod fillets

1 tablespoon vegetable oil

1 onion, finely diced

1 fennel bulb, outside layer removed, then finely chopped

3 garlic cloves, crushed to a paste with a little sea salt

½ teaspoon chili powder

1 teaspoon ground coriander

1 teaspoon ground cumin

1 teaspoon ground turmeric

14 oz canned chopped tomatoes

1 teaspoon superfine sugar

⅔ cup (5 oz) fat-free Greek yogurt

1 teaspoon garam masala

3 tomatoes, roughly chopped

2 mild green peppers, seeded and roughly chopped

handful of baby spinach, washed

Preheat the oven to 425°F.

Place the flour on a plate, then dip in the cod to coat both sides, shaking off any excess.

Heat the oil in an ovenproof frying pan over high heat, brown the cod on both sides, remove and set aside.

Into the same pan, add the onion, fennel, and garlic and cook gently for 10–12 minutes until the vegetables have softened, but have little or no color. Add all the spices except for the garam masala and cook for 2 minutes.

Add the canned tomatoes and sugar, increase the heat, and cook for 10 minutes to thicken, then fold in the yogurt, and stir to combine. Return the cod to the pan together with the garam masala, chopped tomatoes, and chiles. Cover, place in the oven, and cook for 12 minutes.

Remove from the oven, take out the cod fillets and keep warm in a serving dish. Add the spinach to the sauce and cook until wilted. Check the seasoning, then spoon over the cod and serve.

Chicken and bacon dhal

Per serving

365 cals   7.4g fiber

7.7g fat   2g salt

1.5g saturated fat

6.4g sugar   **2.8g fat per 100g**

I know that dhal dishes are normally associated with vegetarianism, but I reckon they're great for meat dishes as well. Serve this with a salad.

Serves 4

1½ cups (10 oz) yellow split peas, rinsed

1 teaspoon ground turmeric

1 teaspoon ground cumin

1 teaspoon ground coriander

¼ teaspoon ground fennel

1 teaspoon sea salt

½ teaspoon ground white pepper

4 curry leaves

1 tablespoon vegetable oil

2 slices Canadian bacon, fat removed

4 skinless, boneless chicken thighs, each cut into three

1 onion, finely chopped

4 garlic cloves, crushed to a paste with a little sea salt

1 teaspoon fresh grated ginger

1 teaspoon brown mustard seeds

5 oz extra fine green beans

¼ winter (Savoy) cabbage, finely shredded

½ teaspoon garam masala

3 scallions, finely sliced

1 mild green pepper, seeded and finely sliced (optional)

Put the split peas in a saucepan and cover with water extending 1 inch above the peas. Bring to a boil, reduce the heat, and simmer for 5 minutes.

Add the turmeric, cumin, coriander, fennel, salt, pepper, and curry leaves, then cover with a lid, and simmer for 1 hour, skimming off any scum from time to time. Make sure that the split peas are tender, but haven't completely collapsed.

Meanwhile, 20 minutes before the end of the dhal cooking time, heat the oil in a wok or saucepan, then add the bacon and chicken, and cook over medium heat for 12 minutes. Remove, and set aside to keep warm.

Add the onion, garlic, ginger, and mustard seeds to the chicken pan and cook gently for 10 minutes before adding the beans, cabbage, and 3 tablespoons of water. Cook for 2 minutes, then return the chicken and bacon to the pan, together with the split pea mixture. Stir to combine, then fold in the garam masala and check the seasoning.

Scatter the surface with scallions and chili if desired.

Lamb stew on the quick

Per serving

420 cals   3.2g fiber
12.6g fat   0.6g salt
5.1g saturated fat
4.8g sugar   **2.9g fat per 100g**

This is so simple, but so tasty, and it's literally going to take you only minutes to have supper on the table. Lamb is not cheap nowadays, so I've gone for one of its best-value cuts, but you will have to slice it thinly to save your molars. Serve with new potatoes.

Serves 6

1 lb lamb shoulder neck, trimmed of
    any sinews or fat
spray of olive oil
1 onion, finely diced
4 garlic cloves, crushed to a paste
    with a little sea salt
1 tablespoon toasted cumin seeds
3 anchovy fillets, roughly chopped
a pinch of crushed red pepper flakes
½ teaspoon ground rosemary, or very
    finely chopped rosemary needles
¾ cup (6 fl oz) white wine
14 oz canned chopped tomatoes
14 oz canned green kidney (flageolet)
    beans, drained and rinsed
2 tablespoons chopped parsley
1 lb pappardelle or other large pasta

Cut the lamb fillet crosswise into ¼-inch slices across the grain, spray with a fine film of oil, then fry in a large frying pan over high heat for 1 minute on each side. Remove and set aside to keep warm. You may have to fry in batches to accommodate all the lamb.

In the same pan, cook the onion over medium heat for 8–10 minutes, without it coloring too much, then add the garlic, cumin, anchovy, red pepper flakes, and rosemary. Stir to combine, and cook for another 3 minutes until the anchovy breaks down.

Add the white wine, and boil vigorously until most of the liquid has evaporated, then add the tomatoes and cook for 10 minutes. Add the beans along with the lamb and any accumulated juices. Heat through for 5 minutes, but do not let it boil. Season and fold in the parsley.

Meanwhile, cook the pasta according to the manufacturer's instructions and serve with the stew.

Tip

This recipe works equally well with chicken or pork tenderloin, although you may have to cook the meat for a little longer depending on how thick you cut it.

Cajun shrimp with green beans and cilantro

Per serving
124 cals   2.4g fiber
4.3g fat   1.8g salt
0.5g saturated fat
9.5g sugar   **2g fat per 100g**

I love Cajun spice mixes, and this blend works well with other shellfish, white fish, chicken, or pork; you can make the paste in larger quantities if you like. The shrimp go well with rice or new potatoes, and they also make a great filling for a tortilla wrap, or as a topping for pancakes.

Serves 4

CAJUN PASTE:

1 tablespoon sweet paprika

1 teaspoon onion salt

1 teaspoon garlic salt

1 teaspoon chili powder or cayenne
    pepper

½ teaspoon ground ginger

2 tablespoons ground cumin

1 teaspoon ground coriander

1 teaspoon ground cardamom

1 red onion, roughly chopped

1 tablespoon vegetable oil

3 garlic cloves, roughly chopped

24 raw tiger shrimp, shelled and
    deveined

6 oz extra-fine green beans, cut into
    1-inch pieces

spray of vegetable oil

8 cherry tomatoes, halved

1 red onion, finely sliced

juice and grated zest of 1 lime

2 teaspoons honey

½ bunch of cilantro, leaves only

For the Cajun paste, simply blend all the ingredients in a food processor. Thin half the paste with a little water, and use to marinate the shrimp, tossing to combine. Leave covered for 20 minutes.

Cook the beans in plenty of boiling, salted water for 4 minutes. Drain, discard the water and set aside.

Spray a large frying pan with oil, add the remaining paste and fry until fragrant, about 2 minutes, stirring continuously. Add the shrimp and cook for 2 minutes. Then add the tomatoes and onion, and cook for another 2 minutes, stirring frequently.

Fold in the beans, lime juice and zest, honey, and cilantro, and toss to combine. Cook for 1–2 minutes until everything is piping hot.

Smoked haddock and salmon biryani

Per serving	
411 cals	3.6g fiber
13.6g fat	2.4g salt
6g saturated fat	
15.4g sugar	**3g fat per 100g**

This recipe is loosely based on kedgeree, but with a few more Indian spices added and a different cooking technique. It's a lovely one-pot dinner-party dish that has loads of flavor. All you need is a salad to go with it.

Serves 6

1 tablespoon vegetable oil

2 onions, finely chopped

4 garlic cloves, crushed to a paste with a little sea salt

1 teaspoon fresh grated ginger

1 teaspoon ground coriander

1 teaspoon ground cumin

2 green cardamom pods, lightly crushed

1-inch cinnamon stick

1 teaspoon ground turmeric

½ teaspoon chili powder

1 teaspoon yellow mustard seeds

generous cup (8 oz) long-grain or basmati rice, rinsed

2½ cups (20 fl oz) chicken or fish stock

1¼ cups (10 fl oz) light coconut milk

1¼ cups (10 oz) fat-free Greek yogurt

⅔ cup (4 oz) frozen green peas, defrosted

1 large zucchini, finely sliced

⅔ cup (4 oz) dried apricots, finely chopped

8 oz natural smoked haddock fillets, skin removed, cut into 1-inch dice

7 oz salmon fillet, cut into 1-inch dice

2 tablespoons chopped cilantro, leaves and stalks

2 green peppers, seeded and thinly sliced

Preheat the oven to 375°F.

In an ovenproof saucepan with a lid, heat the oil over medium heat, then add the onion, garlic, and ginger and cook gently for 10 minutes, stirring from time to time.

Add all the spices and stir to combine, cooking for 1 minute. Measure the rice using a measuring cup as you add it to the pan with the spiced onions. Then measure one and half times as much stock as rice, and add this to the pan as well. Bring to a boil, cover with a circle of parchment paper, then a lid, and pop in the oven for 15 minutes. When it's ready, stir through with a fork.

Meanwhile, bring the coconut milk and yogurt to a boil in a pan, then reduce the heat, and add the peas, zucchini, apricots and the haddock and salmon. Cook for 6–8 minutes. Season, then fold in the cilantro and green peppers.

Fold the fish mixture into the rice, and check the seasoning.

Roast butternut squash, leek, and tomato risotto

Per serving

296 cals

4g fat

0.9g saturated fat

15.5g sugar

8.1g fiber

1.8g salt

0.7g fat per 100g

Risotto needs cheese, or does it? I found that, by adding a vegetable purée, we can compensate for the lack of a cheesy flavor. This recipe allows for many vegetable options.

Serves 6

1 small butternut squash, peeled, seeded and cut into 1-inch dice

4 sprigs of thyme

½ head of garlic, cloves separated, but unpeeled

2 onions, peeled and cut into 8 wedges

spray of olive oil

25 fl oz vegetable stock

2 teaspoons olive oil

2 sticks of celery, finely sliced

1 carrot, peeled and finely diced

1 bay leaf

1⅓ cups (8 oz) arborio rice

2 leeks, washed and shredded finely

⅔ cup (4 oz) frozen fava beans, defrosted

⅔ cup (4 oz) frozen green peas, defrosted

3 tomatoes, seeded and finely diced

Preheat the oven to 400°F.

Put the butternut squash, thyme, garlic, and onions in a bowl and spray with olive oil. Toss to coat, then season and put into a baking pan and roast for 30 minutes, stirring from time to time.

Meanwhile, heat the stock to boiling in a saucepan.

In another saucepan, heat the oil, then add the celery, carrot, and bay leaf. Cook gently for 10–12 minutes to soften the vegetables. Add the rice and half the leeks, and toss to combine. Add one ladleful of stock and, stirring constantly, cook until the liquid has all but evaporated and been soaked up by the rice. Then add another and so on until the rice is tender, about 18–20 minutes.

Meanwhile, when the squash is cooked, remove from the oven, pop the garlic out of their skins, then put half of the roast vegetables and garlic into a food processor and blend until smooth.

Eight minutes before the risotto has finished cooking, add the purée to the pan, together with the rest of the roast vegetables, the remaining leeks, fava beans, and peas. Two minutes before the end of the cooking time, add the diced tomatoes and season to taste.

Tip

It's important, to obtain the risotto's distinctive creamy texture, to add the stock little by little. If you're not sure whether the rice is cooked, just take a teaspoon and try it; you're looking for a tiny bite to the rice.

Pork with celeriac and apple purée

Per serving
283 cals   6.9g fiber
8.1g fat   1g salt
1.9g saturated fat
10.6g sugar   **1.8g fat per 100g**

I've always been a massive fan of pork, which is a low-fat meat, and the combination of celeriac and apples creates a perfect partnership. Celeriac is an underused vegetable, partly I'm sure because of its appearance, which tends to scare all but the keenest cooks; the best plan is to think of celeriac simply as a knobbly potato, and to cook it in the same way.

Serves 6

1 tablespoon olive oil

1½ lb pork tenderloin, trimmed of any fat

1 tablespoon Dijon mustard

1 tablespoon redcurrant jelly

¾ cup (6 fl oz) red wine

1 celeriac, peeled and cut into 1-inch dice

2 russet potatoes, peeled and cut into 1-inch dice

2 Granny Smith apples, peeled, cored and cut into 1-inch dice

1 tablespoon yellow mustard seeds

½ cup (4 fl oz) chicken stock

2 teaspoons finely chopped sage leaves

Preheat the oven to 400°F.

Heat the oil in a frying pan and brown the pork all over. Remove from the pan, and allow to cool slightly before painting all over with Dijon mustard. Place in the oven and cook for 15–20 minutes.

Meanwhile, add the redcurrant jelly and wine to the pork browning pan, and simmer gently until the jelly melts.

At the same time, place the celeriac, potatoes, and apple in a pan of boiling salted water and cook for 12–15 minutes, until the potato and celeriac are tender. Drain and dry well, then mash, pass through a fine sieve, or pulse in a food processor until smooth. Set aside and keep warm.

Meanwhile, it's back to the sauce. Add the mustard seeds, chicken stock, and sage to the red wine reduction, and cook until reduced by one-third. Season.

Remove the pork from the oven and allow to rest for at least 5 minutes. Scrape any juices from the roasting pan into the sauce. Carve the pork into thick slices on the diagonal. Serve the sauce spooned over the pork, alongside a nice dollop of celeriac and apple purée.

Tip

If preparing the celeriac and apple in advance, place the raw, peeled dice in acidulated water until ready to cook, to prevent them from going brown.

Pearl barley and wild mushroom pilaf

Per serving
414 cals   2.8g fiber
5.3g fat   2.2g salt
1g saturated fat
4.9g sugar   **1.1g fat per 100g**

I love the texture of pearl barley. It has a lovely feel about it, and makes a low-GI substitute for rice. It's often used in soups and stews, but you now see pearl barley more regularly in dishes like this and risotto.

Serves 4

1½ cups (11 oz) pearl barley, washed and soaked in cold water for 1 hour

1 oz dried cep mushrooms (porcini), soaked in boiling water for 30 minutes

1 tablespoon olive oil

1 onion, finely chopped

2 garlic cloves, crushed to a paste with a little sea salt

1 teaspoon thyme leaves

2 bay leaves

1 celery stick, finely chopped

1 carrot, peeled and cut into ¼-inch dice

scant 2 cups (15 fl oz) vegetable stock

1¼ cups (10 fl oz) red wine

14 oz mixed wild mushrooms, cleaned and cut in half if too large

1 teaspoon ground black pepper

2 teaspoons Maggi seasoning (optional)

2 handfuls of baby spinach leaves, washed

Drain the pearl barley and set aside.

Carefully remove the soaked ceps without disturbing the soaking liquid too much. Roughly chop the mushrooms and set aside. Strain the mushroom soaking liquid through a coffee filter, muslin, or a very fine sieve to remove any gritty particles, then set aside.

Preheat the oven to 350°F.

Heat the oil in an ovenproof saucepan, and cook the onion over medium heat for 8–10 minutes until softened. Add the garlic, thyme, bay leaves, celery, and carrot and cook for another 3 minutes.

Meanwhile, heat the vegetable stock and red wine with the reserved mushroom liquid until just below boiling point.

Add both the fresh and soaked mushrooms to the onion mixture and cook over high heat for 3 minutes. Add the barley, black pepper, and heated stock, stir to combine, then bring to a boil, cover, and place in the preheated oven for 35 minutes. By this stage, all the liquid should have been absorbed.

Take out of the oven, remove the lid and, over very low heat, stir in the Maggi seasoning, if using, and the baby spinach. Stir until the spinach has wilted. Check the seasoning, then serve piping hot.

Tip

I'm a great fan of Maggi liquid seasoning in soups and stews. It's like a vegetarian version of Worcestershire sauce, and adds that little *je ne sais quoi*, but beware, it does contain MSG.

Vegetable tagine

Per serving
301 cals   9.6g fiber
9.3g fat   1.8g salt
1.2g saturated fat
27.1g sugar   **1.6g fat per 100g**

Ever since I filmed a TV series in Morocco, I've been hooked on their use of spices, and here we turn humble vegetables into a sumptuous vegetarian feast.

Serves 8

2 teaspoons olive oil

1 lb onions, half grated and half cut into chunky dice

½ head of garlic, peeled and crushed with sea salt

½ tablespoon ground ginger

½ teaspoon ground black pepper

½ teaspoon ground cinnamon

1 cup (6 oz) dried apricots, soaked in a little water

¾ cup (3 oz) flaked almonds

⅓ cup (2 oz) golden raisins or raisins

1 teaspoon honey

2½ cups (20 fl oz) tomato juice

2½ cups (20 fl oz) vegetable stock

10 oz potatoes, peeled and cut into 1-inch chunks

2 green bell peppers, seeded and cut into 1-inch chunks

10 oz pumpkin or butternut squash, peeled, seeded and cut into 1-inch chunks

14 oz canned chopped tomatoes

14 oz canned chickpeas, drained and rinsed

2 large zucchini, cut into 1-inch chunks

10 oz cauliflower florets

10 oz fresh or frozen peas

¾ cup (1 oz) chopped cilantro

Heat the olive oil in a large, ovenproof casserole dish. When it's hot, add the grated onion, garlic, and spices and gently cook until the onions are soft and translucent, about 6–8 minutes. Take care not to brown the onions, or scorch the spices.

Add the remaining onions, apricots and their soaking water, the almonds, raisins, honey, tomato juice, and vegetable stock. Bring to a boil, reduce the heat, and allow to simmer until the sauce has reduced by one-third.

Add the vegetables in order of cooking time: start with the potatoes and bell peppers and gently cook for approximately 12 minutes, then add the pumpkin or squash, canned tomatoes, and chickpeas, cook for 8 minutes, then add the zucchini, cauliflower florets, and the peas. Continue to cook until all the vegetables are tender, about another 10 minutes.

Serve immediately, sprinkled with cilantro.

Roast lemon chicken with root vegetables

Per serving

409 cals   7.4g fiber

13.5g fat   0.6g salt

3.4g saturated fat

17.1g sugar   **2.4g fat per 100g**

There is a bit of a dilemma here, as most of the fat is in the chicken skin, which will be reduced by roasting, rendering the skin very crisp and very delicious—but you know better, so remove the skin before carving, and drain all the fat from the roasting juices. This is easily done if you have a gravy fat separator, otherwise pour the juices into a glass measuring cup, which will enable you to see the fats and skim them off; you can fish out any small bubbles by dragging a piece of paper towel over the surface.

Serves 4

grated zest and juice of 1 unwaxed lemon

2 garlic cloves, crushed to a paste with a little sea salt

3 sprigs of rosemary, 1 stripped of its leaves and finely chopped

pinch of crushed red pepper flakes

$1/8$ teaspoon ground black pepper

3¼ lb free-range roasting chicken, (skin removed after cooking)

12 baby onions, peeled

½ butternut squash (approx. 12 oz), peeled, seeded and cut into ¾-inch dice

12 baby carrots (approx. 10 oz), scrubbed

8 baby leeks (approx. 14 oz), washed and trimmed

8 new potatoes (approx. 7 oz), halved

6 baby zucchini (approx. 10 oz), halved lengthwise

2 teaspoons olive oil

Preheat the oven to 400°F.

Mash the lemon zest and juice with the garlic, chopped rosemary leaves, chile, and black pepper, and spread over and inside the chicken.

In a bowl, combine all the vegetables with the oil, and season with salt and ground black pepper. Tip them into a roasting pan, make a little well in the center, and place the chicken in this well.

Roast the chicken and vegetables in the oven for 1¼ hours, turning the vegetables frequently. Remove the chicken to a warm place, and allow to rest for 15 minutes. With a slotted spoon, lift the vegetables into a serving bowl.

Skim off any fat from the roasting juices, and add 4 tablespoons of water to the roasting pan. Stir to remove any pan residue, pour these juices over the carved chicken, and serve with the vegetables.

Tip

Feel free to mix and match the variety of vegetables, making sure that you keep them roughly the same size. If using large carrots, blanch them first for 8–10 minutes.

Roast tenderloin of spiced pork with colorful vegetables

Per serving

403 cals

7.1g fat

2.2g saturated fat

28.5g sugar

7.1g fiber

4.6g salt

1.1g fat per 100g

Pork fillet is still very good value for a quality cut, and it takes big flavors, which is what this dish is about—that and some lovely roast vegetables, of course.

Serves 4

2 x center-cut pork tenderloin, each about 8 oz, trimmed of any fat or sinews

6 tablespoons kecap manis (Indonesian soy sauce)

2 tablespoons mirin (Japanese rice wine) or dry sherry

1 teaspoon five spice powder

¼ teaspoon red food coloring (optional)

2 garlic cloves, crushed to a paste with a little sea salt

1 teaspoon hot chili sauce

1 teaspoon fresh grated ginger

THE VEGETABLES:

1 red bell pepper, seeded and cut into 1-inch pieces

½ butternut squash, peeled, seeded and cut into 1-inch pieces

8 new potatoes, halved

2 zucchini, cut into 1-inch rounds

1 leek, washed and cut into 1-inch rounds

1 red onion, peeled and cut into 8 wedges

spray of vegetable oil

8 garlic cloves, unpeeled

2 tablespoons rice vinegar

2 tablespoons superfine sugar

Place the pork tenderloin in a shallow dish. In a small bowl, stir together the kecap manis, mirin, five spice powder, red food coloring (if using), garlic, chili sauce, and grated ginger. Pour over the pork and marinate for 4 hours, turning from time to time.

Preheat the oven to 375°F.

Place all the vegetables in a bowl, spray with oil, and season with salt and pepper. Mix well, then put in a roasting pan, and top with the pork tenderloin. Place in the oven and roast for 50 minutes, adding the garlic cloves after 20 minutes. During the cooking, baste every so often with the marinade.

Remove the meat and rest in a warm place, then toss the vegetables in the vinegar and sugar, and return to the oven for 8 minutes.

Carve the pork, and serve on a platter of the roast vegetables.

Spiced salmon and shrimp with yogurt and white beans

Per serving

234 cals   6.4g fiber

6.9g fat   0.5g salt

1.2g saturated fat

4.6g sugar   **2.1g fat per 100g**

Salmon is such a good vehicle for transporting strong flavors; here I've gone for some Moroccan influence, with all you require on one plate.

Serves 4

3 garlic cloves, crushed to a paste with a little sea salt

1 tablespoon ground coriander

1 teaspoon ground cumin

1 teaspoon ground fennel

1 teaspoon ground turmeric

1 tablespoon olive oil

1 tablespoon water

16 raw tiger shrimp, peeled

3 oz salmon fillets

28 oz canned cannellini beans, drained

½ cucumber, peeled and seeded and cut into ¼-inch dice

1 tablespoon chopped mint

3 tablespoons chopped cilantro

¾ cup (6 oz) fat-free Greek yogurt

spray of olive oil

8 cherry tomatoes halved horizontally

Combine the garlic with the spices, oil, and water to make a paste. Rub the shrimp and the salmon fillets with half the paste, massaging it well into the flesh. Allow the flavors to develop for 20 minutes.

Meanwhile, mix the remaining paste with the cannellini beans, cucumber, mint, cilantro and yogurt.

Spray a nonstick frying pan with a film of oil, pan-fry the salmon for 2 minutes on each side, remove and set aside to keep warm, then repeat with the shrimp, cooking for 1 minute on each side. Add to the salmon and keep warm.

Add the bean mix to the fish pan, and cook for 5 minutes to warm through.

Serve the salmon and the shrimp on a bed of beans, and scatter each plate with 4 tomato halves.

Tip

This would be a lovely picnic dish—cook the salmon and shrimp in the usual way and allow to cool. There is no need to cook the beans.

Spicy shrimp balls in a tomato and cilantro sauce

Per serving

245 cals   3.1g fiber

3.3g fat   2.8g salt

0.5g saturated fat

13.7g sugar   **0.6g fat per 100g**

Always try to eat at least two portions of fish each week, which is easier said than done according to the statistics. I would serve this with spaghetti or rice.

Serves 4

SAUCE:

28 oz canned chopped tomatoes

2 teaspoons olive oil

1 onion, finely chopped

3 garlic cloves, crushed to a paste
    with a little sea salt

3 small dried chiles

juice and zest of 1 orange

12 cherry tomatoes

½ bunch of cilantro, roughly chopped

2 handfuls of baby spinach, washed

2 teaspoons superfine sugar

1 tablespoon nam pla (fish sauce)

SHRIMP BALLS:

1½ lb raw shrimp, shelled, deveined
    and roughly chopped

2 garlic cloves, roughly chopped

3 small red Thai chiles, roughly
    chopped

1 teaspoon ground ginger

grated zest and juice of 1 lime

2 tablespoons chopped cilantro

5 scallions, roughly chopped

2 tablespoons chopped mint

1 tablespoon cornstarch

1 tablespoon nam pla (fish sauce)

1 egg white, lightly beaten

For the sauce, blend the canned tomatoes in a food processor until smooth. Set aside.

Heat the oil in a saucepan, then over medium heat, cook the onion, garlic and chiles for 8–10 minutes until soft, but not colored. Add the orange juice and zest, and continue to cook until most of the liquid has evaporated. Add the puréed tomatoes, bring to a boil, then reduce the heat and simmer for 12 minutes.

To make the shrimp balls, pulse the chopped shrimp with the garlic, chile, ginger, lime juice and zest in a food processor until semi-smooth, but with some texture remaining. Transfer the shrimp mixture to a bowl, add the cilantro, scallions, mint, cornstarch, nam pla, and egg white, and mix thoroughly.

With wet hands, roll the mixture into small balls of differing sizes (in other words I'm not too fussed whether they are all the same size). When finished, pop them all into the tomato sauce and cook for 6 minutes before adding the cherry tomatoes, chopped cilantro, baby spinach, sugar, and nam pla. Cook for another 4 minutes, check the seasoning and serve.

Pan-fried tuna steaks with soy bok choy

Per serving

259 cals	1.4g fiber
7.4g fat	2.9g salt
1.8g saturated fat	
6.1g sugar	**2.4g fat per 100g**

Fresh tuna is classified as an oil-rich fish, so it contains good amounts of omega-3 fats. Plus, it's packed with protein.

Serves 4

4 tablespoons Japanese soy sauce

4 tablespoons mirin (Japanese rice wine)

4 tablespoons sake

2 teaspoons honey

1 teaspoon fresh grated ginger

juice of 1 lime

4 x 5½ oz tuna steaks

spray of vegetable oil

8 small heads bok choy, halved

4 scallions, finely sliced

1 long red chili, seeded and sliced

Combine the soy sauce, mirin, sake, honey, ginger and lime juice in a bowl, and stir well to combine. Marinate the tuna in this mixture for 40 minutes.

Spray a griddle pan with vegetable oil, and place over medium heat. Drain the tuna (reserving the marinade) and cook for 2 minutes on each side, then remove, and leave to rest in a warm place.

Meanwhile, in a saucepan, bring the marinade to a boil. Add the bok choy and cook over medium heat, turning frequently. It only needs to wilt so 1½–2 minutes should be sufficient.

Place the greens on four warmed plates, top with the tuna steaks and scatter with scallions and chili. Serve immediately with boiled rice.

Jamaican shrimp pepper stew

Per serving

157cals	2.4g fiber
3.8g fat	3.8g salt
1.1g saturated fat	
8g sugar	**0.8g fat per 100g**

Serves 6

1 onion, finely chopped

1 teaspoon crushed garlic

pinch of crushed red pepper flakes

1 tablespoon olive oil

2 red bell peppers, seeded and chopped

1 Scotch Bonnet chile, left whole

2 bay leaves

2 sprigs thyme

½ teaspoon ground allspice

1½ quarts fish or chicken stock

1 sweet potato, peeled and diced

3 tablespoons long-grain rice

1 zucchini, finely diced

6 oz peeled raw tiger shrimp, sliced

1 tablespoon anchovy sauce

2 teaspoons tomato paste

14 oz calaloo (Jamaican spinach)

Place the onion, garlic, and pepper flakes in a large saucepan with the oil and cook gently for 10 minutes, until the onion has softened.

Add the peppers, whole chile, bay leaves, thyme, and allspice, and stir to combine. Cook for 3 minutes.

Add the stock, sweet potato, and rice and bring to a boil, then reduce the heat and simmer for 10 minutes. Stir in the zucchini, shrimp, anchovy essence, and tomato paste and cook for another 3 minutes, before finally adding the calaloo. Fish out the Scotch Bonnet, which is very hot, when you feel the dish has reached the desired chili heat.

Check the seasoning and serve piping hot.

Tip

I'm a fan of calaloo, the West Indian green vegetable which is increasingly available in supermarkets, but if you can't find it, use canned calaloo or defrosted frozen leaf spinach.

Tuna "olives" with fruit

Per serving

389 cals   3g fiber

11.1g fat   0.6g salt

2g saturated fat

15.3g sugar   **2.8g fat per 100g**

When I say "olives" I refer to that famous dish "Beef Olives" and here I'm treating tuna like a piece of meat, but with the advantage that it cooks very quickly. The flavors involved have a north African influence, and tuna, as we know, provides us with omega-3 fatty acids, and is a great protein-rich food.

Serves 4

1 tablespoon olive oil

1 small red onion, finely diced

1 garlic clove, finely chopped

1 pinch crushed red pepper flakes

2 teaspoons harissa

2 tablespoons golden raisins

4 dried apricots

2 teaspoons toasted pine nuts

¼ teaspoon ground cinnamon

1 tablespoon roughly chopped cilantro

2 cups (3 oz) fresh white bread crumbs

4 x 4 oz tuna steaks

spray of olive oil

½ cup (4 fl oz) dry vermouth

2 teaspoons snipped chives

FOR THE SALAD:

4 tomatoes, seeded and diced

½ cucumber, seeded and diced

½ red onion, finely diced

½ teaspoon toasted cumin seeds

1 teaspoon chopped mint

2 tablespoons fat-free Greek yogurt

1 tablespoon lemon juice

Heat the oil in a large frying pan and cook the onion over medium heat for 6–8 minutes until soft, but not colored. Add the garlic, chile, harissa, golden raisins, apricots, and pine nuts, and cook for another 3 minutes, stirring continuously. Allow to cool.

Mix the onion with the cinnamon, cilantro, and bread crumbs, season well, and squeeze together to combine.

Place each tuna steak between two sheets of plastic wrap, and beat gently with a meat mallet or rolling pin until you have doubled the size of the fish—be careful not to tear the flesh. Season well.

Take a quarter of the bread stuffing and squeeze it into a sausage shape, place it on an edge of the tuna, and roll up, securing with a wooden toothpick. Repeat with the other three tuna steaks. Don't worry if some of the filling falls out, you can always push it back in with a teaspoon or your fingers.

Meanwhile make the salad, mixing together everything except the yogurt and lemon juice, which you fold in just before serving, and season.

Heat a frying pan until almost smoking, spray a fine mist of olive oil over the tuna olives, and place them in the frying pan. Cook for 2–3 minutes, turning frequently, then add the vermouth, letting it bubble vigorously for 1 minute.

Fold the yogurt and lemon juice into the salad, and serve alongside the tuna with the chives sprinkled on top.

Tip

This dish would also be great served with the Vegetable tagine (see page 164).

Squid and chickpea stew

Per serving
303 cals   5.5g fiber
7.4g fat   1g salt
1.2g saturated fat
12.2g sugar   **1.6g fat per 100g**

There's something very addictive about a comforting stew and this fishy number checks all the boxes. When cooking squid, you're looking for that vital point between tender and rubbery. You either flash-fry in seconds, or stew for a lengthy period of time. I've chosen the second option. Serve the stew with rice or new potatoes.

Serves 4

2 teaspoons ground cumin

1 teaspoon ground coriander

1 teaspoon ground fennel

½ teaspoon cayenne pepper

½ teaspoon ground allspice

1 tablespoon flour

1 lb squid, cleaned and cut into large bite-size pieces

1 tablespoon olive oil

2 red onions, each cut into 6 wedges

4 garlic cloves, crushed to a paste with a little sea salt

1 carrot, peeled and cut into ½-inch dice

1 red bell pepper, seeded and cut into ½-inch dice

sprig of thyme

2 bay leaves

1 tablespoon anchovy sauce

¾ cup (6 fl oz) dry white wine

14 oz canned chopped tomatoes

2 teaspoons harissa

14 oz canned chickpeas, drained and rinsed

3 tablespoons roughly chopped parsley

In a plastic bag, mix together the spices and flour, then add the squid pieces, and shake to combine. Remove the squid and shake off any excess flour.

Heat the oil in a large saucepan until very hot, then add the squid pieces and fry for 3–4 minutes, turning frequently, until brown. Add the onions, garlic, carrot, bell pepper, thyme, and bay leaves, reduce the heat, and cook for 6–8 minutes until the onion has started to soften.

Add the anchovy sauce, wine, tomatoes, and harissa and bring to a boil. Reduce the heat, then cover with a lid, and simmer gently for 1 hour, stirring from time to time. Test the squid to see whether it is tender; if not, cook until it's done.

Fold in the chickpeas and parsley and season to taste. Cook for 3–5 minutes to heat through.

Tip

When cutting up the squid, make the pieces quite large as it does tend to shrink during cooking.

Broiled chili squid

Per serving

143 cals	0.6g fiber
5.3g fat	0.7g salt
1g saturated fat	
1.9g sugar	**2.8g fat per 100g**

This is a very simple dish once you've mastered the art of preparing squid, but the easy answer to that is to get your fish market to do it for you. Please don't buy frozen squid as they tend to be pumped up with water, and won't broil well; fresh is definitely best. Serve with steamed new potatoes and salad.

Serves 4

2 roasted red peppers from a jar, drained well and patted dry

2 red peppers, seeds and stem removed

½ teaspoon crushed red pepper flakes

½ teaspoon smoked paprika

1 teaspoon thyme leaves

2 garlic cloves, roughly chopped

2 scallions, roughly sliced

½ bunch of cilantro, leaves and stalks

1 tablespoon olive oil

1¼ lb cleaned squid

spray of vegetable oil

Place all the ingredients, apart from the squid and the oil, in a food processor and blend until smooth. Place in a bowl.

Cut open the squid tubes and give them a quick rinse, then pat dry. Lay the squid flat on your work surface, with the inside facing up. Then, with a sharp knife, cut three-quarters through the flesh in a tight, cross-hatch effect; this helps to keep the squid tender, and also looks cute when it's cooked. Cut each tube into three.

Place the squid in the red pepper marinade, and leave for 30 minutes.

Spray a little oil onto a griddle pan and get the pan really hot. In batches, place the squid cut-side down on the hot pan, and cook for 45 seconds on each side. When you turn the squid over, the pieces will roll up into tubes.

Serve immediately.

Per serving

145 cals	0g fiber
2g fat	0.2g salt
0.4g saturated fat	
0.7g sugar	**1g fat per 100g**

Spiced-up monkfish

This is a great way to put more flavor into a meaty fish; the marinade is certainly not for the faint-hearted, or for delicate fish. Serve the monkfish with salad, or the fruity low-fat jewelled couscous on page 216.

Serves 4

1 tablespoon sweet paprika

1 teaspoon ground cumin

1 teaspoon ground coriander

½ teaspoon garam masala

½ teaspoon ground black pepper

½ teaspoon ground turmeric

4 tablespoons rice vinegar

2 tablespoons harissa

1 teaspoon garlic purée

1 teaspoon ginger purée

4 x 6 oz monkfish steaks

spray of vegetable oil

Combine the first ten ingredients in a bowl then spread the marinade over the fish. Leave for 3 hours for the flavors to develop.

Spray vegetable oil into a large frying pan and cook the monkfish for 5 minutes on each side.

A casserole of sweet potatoes, spinach, and sweet peppers

Per serving
204 cals
2.8g fat
0.4g saturated fat
12.8g sugar

7.1g fiber
0.5g salt

0.8g fat per 100g

A lovely vegetarian stew with a few superfoods enhanced by great depth of flavor. I love sweet potatoes, but obviously you can add whatever vegetables you like, as long as you start with the suggested onion and spice base.

Serves 4

2 teaspoons canola oil
1 red onion, cut into 8 wedges
3 garlic cloves, roughly chopped
2 long red peppers, seeded and finely sliced
1 teaspoon sweet paprika
½ teaspoon ground cumin
½ teaspoon ground fennel
2 sweet potatoes, peeled and cut into
 8 wedges each
8 peppadew peppers, drained and halved
14 oz canned chopped tomatoes
14 oz canned cannellini beans
2 tablespoons chopped parsley
2 handfuls baby leaf spinach, washed
2 tablespoons fat-free Greek yogurt

Heat the oil in a large saucepan, then add the onion, garlic, and chili and cook over medium heat for 8–10 minutes to soften, but not color the onions.

Stir in the spices, then add the sweet potato, peppers, and canned tomatoes. Cook, uncovered, for 20 minutes, stirring from time to time. Season.

Fold in the cannellini beans, parsley, and spinach, and cook for about 5 minutes until the beans are hot and the spinach has wilted. (You will have to be careful when adding the spinach as it can easily end up over your stove top…fold it in carefully!)

Serve in four warm bowls, and top with a little yogurt.

Red snapper with roast cherry tomatoes, garlic, and basil

Per serving
213 cals
5.6g fat
1.1g saturated fat
3.9g sugar

1.5g fiber
0.8g salt

1.8g fat per 100g

I'm a converted fan of red snapper, especially the variety known as Bourgeois, but have come to realize that it needs big flavors as it's a really meaty fish. As with most fish, red snapper mustn't be overcooked, so this dish is perfect for a fast supper, and a delicious and healthy one, too. Serve with new potatoes.

Serves 4

9 oz red cherry tomatoes
9 oz yellow cherry tomatoes
12 garlic cloves, peeled
1 tablespoon olive oil
4 x 6 oz snapper fillets, skinned and cut
 into 1-inch dice
1 tablespoon Lilliput capers, drained
1 tablespoon sherry vinegar
16 basil leaves, torn

Preheat the oven to 375°F.

Put the tomatoes, garlic, and olive oil in a bowl, season with salt and pepper, and toss to coat. Tip into a roasting pan, place in the oven and cook for 25 minutes, stirring from time to time.

Add the fish pieces, season and cook for another 10–12 minutes before adding capers, vinegar, and basil leaves. Toss gently to combine and wilt the basil leaves, taking care not to break up the fish.

I love noodles

Per serving
366 cals   5.7g fiber
9.2g fat   1.7g salt
0.8g saturated fat
10.8g sugar   **1.9g fat per 100g**

I say "I love noodles" rather than describe this as "pork noodles" because this is a one-size-fits-all dish: you could substitute beef tenderloin, chicken breast, shrimp, or squid as the main source of protein. And, as a bonus, you'll find this will be a winner with the whole family.

Serves 4

1 lb fresh egg noodles

spray of vegetable oil

11 oz pork tenderloin, trimmed and shaved very thinly

2 teaspoons vegetable oil

4 scallions, sliced on the diagonal

1 green bell pepper, seeded and cut into 1-inch pieces

1 carrot, peeled and shaved into long ribbons with a potato peeler

1 zucchini, shaved into long ribbons with a potato peeler

4 oz button mushrooms, cleaned and quartered

2 garlic cloves, thinly sliced

1 teaspoon fresh grated ginger

½ teaspoon ground Sichuan peppercorns

2 tablespoons oyster sauce

2 tablespoons low-sodium soy sauce

2 teaspoons grated palm sugar or honey

6 oz sugar snap peas or snow peas

3 bok choy, cut in half

Pour boiling water over the noodles to cover and leave for 1 minute. Then, without burning your fingers, separate the noodles, drain and set aside to keep warm.

Over very high heat, warm a wok until smoking before spraying with oil, then quickly and in batches pan-fry the pork tenderloin until brown, about 2 minutes. Remove and set aside to keep warm.

Add the oil to the wok, heat to high, then stir-fry the scallions, bell pepper, and carrot for 2 minutes. Add 2 tablespoons water, followed by the zucchini, mushrooms, garlic, ginger, and pepper, and cook for another minute.

Add the oyster sauce, soy sauce, palm sugar or honey, sugar snap peas, and bok choy, along with the noodles and pork. Toss for about 2 minutes, until the bok choy has wilted, and the noodles and pork are warmed through.

Serve in four warm bowls.

Sweet and not-so-sour chicken

Per serving

204 cals   2.7g fiber

6.9g fat   2.5g salt

1g saturated fat

13.1g sugar   **2g fat per 100g**

This is a really easy and exceptionally delicious chicken dish that should please the whole family. Don't be tempted to use canned pineapple—it just won't be good enough, and you'll miss out on the crunch of fresh fruit.

Serves 4

2 tablespoons vegetable oil

1 onion, thinly sliced

3 garlic cloves, thinly sliced

2 skinless, boneless chicken breasts, cut into thin slivers

1 red bell pepper, seeded and cut into 1-inch pieces

1 tablespoon nam pla (fish sauce)

2 tablespoons oyster sauce

2 tablespoons tomato ketchup

2 x ¾-inch slices of fresh pineapple, peeled, cored and cut into ¾-inch cubes

3 ripe tomatoes, each roughly cut into about six pieces

½ cucumber, peeled, seeded and cut into ¾-inch cubes

1 tablespoon low-sodium soy sauce

8 mint leaves, shredded

Heat a wok, add the oil and cook the onion and garlic over high heat for 3–4 minutes, stirring constantly, until the onions start to brown.

Add the chicken slivers and bell peppers and cook for 2 minutes, stirring continuously. Add the three sauces, together with the pineapple, tomatoes, and cucumber. Toss vigorously to combine, and cook for 2 minutes.

Season with soy sauce, garnish with mint, and serve with rice.

Tip

"What do I do with the rest of the pineapple?" I hear you say. Broiled pineapple slices with honey and fresh lime would be my suggestion.

Vietnamese beef and noodles

Per serving

306 cals   2.3g fiber

5.7g fat   0.9g salt

2.4g saturated fat

3.3g sugar   **0.8g fat per 100g**

I would hate to upset the Vietnamese by playing with their beef dish Pho Bo, but mine is loosely based on this classic. On a low-fat diet we can't eat a lot of beef, but this one passes muster. It's a great way to eat—soupy, noodley, beefy.

Serves 4

1¼ quarts beef stock, homemade if possible

2½ cups (20 fl oz) water

1 stalk of lemongrass, left whole, bruised

2 Thai red peppers, left whole

2 kaffir lime leaves

4 garlic cloves, smashed

bunch of cilantro, stalks and leaves

1 star anise

4-inch piece of ginger, thinly sliced

11½ oz beef fillet, trimmed and thinly sliced

spray of oil

6 oz dried thin vermicelli (rice noodles)

4 oz snow peas, thinly sliced lengthwise

12 button mushrooms, quartered

2 bok choy, roughly cut

16 mint leaves, shredded

2 tablespoons lime juice

1 tablespoon nam pla (fish sauce)

scant ½ cup (3 oz) bean sprouts

6 scallions, finely sliced

thinly sliced red peppers and lime wedges, to serve

In a large pot, heat the beef stock and water with the lemongrass, chiles, lime leaves, garlic, cilantro stalks, star anise, and ginger. Bring to a boil, reduce the heat, and simmer for 20 minutes. Strain, discarding the solids, and return to the saucepan.

Heat a large frying pan. Season the beef, spray with a light misting of oil, and pan-fry over high heat for about 45 seconds on each side. Set aside to keep warm.

Pour boiling water over the noodles, leave to soften for about 1 minute, then drain, and divide between four warm bowls.

Meanwhile, add the snow peas, mushrooms, bok choy, mint, and cilantro leaves to the stock, and cook for 1 minute. Stir in the lime juice and fish sauce.

Scatter the bean sprouts and scallions over the noodles, and top with slices of beef, then spoon over the vegetable stock. Serve with extra chile and lime wedges.

Peppered chicken with tomatoes and zucchini

Per serving
168 cals   3g fiber
4.8g fat   0.2g salt
1g saturated fat
8.9g sugar   **1.3g fat per 100g**

This is another very simple chicken dish, concentrating on big flavor—this time it's pepper, with a glancing visit to India. It's an all-in-one dish, although you may want to serve it with rice or new potatoes.

Serves 4

8 skinless, boneless chicken thighs, cut into 3
2 teaspoons vegetable oil
2 teaspoons freshly ground black pepper
4 garlic cloves, finely chopped
1 teaspoon fresh grated ginger
2 onions, cut into wedges
4 tomatoes, roughly chopped
1 teaspoon ground turmeric
1 teaspoon garam masala
2 large zucchini, cut into ¾-inch rounds
½ cup (4 fl oz) water
3 tablespoons chopped cilantro

Toss the chicken thigh meat in the oil, then coat in half the pepper and season with salt.

Heat a saucepan and cook the chicken gently to color but not scorch (spices become bitter if the heat is too intense). Brown all over, then remove the chicken and set aside.

Add the garlic, ginger, and onions to the pan, and fry over medium heat for 8–10 minutes to lightly color and soften the onion. Add the remaining black pepper, tomatoes, turmeric, garam masala, zucchini, and the water. Cook for 5 minutes, then return the chicken to the pan, and cook for 10 minutes longer, before checking the seasoning and folding in the cilantro.

Tip

If your tomatoes are a fairly tasteless variety, you might do better to add 14 oz canned chopped tomatoes, in which case you won't need the water.

Fast and furious shrimp

Per serving

51 cals	0g fiber
0.6g fat	0.9g salt
0.1g saturated fat	
0.1g sugar	**0.9g fat per 100g**

I say "furious," because you're getting a chili whammy. They are delicious hot or cold—served with a salad, for example, or slapped between slices of bread. I'll sometimes have them ready in the refrigerator to be picked at from time to time.

Serves 4

32 raw tiger shrimp, peeled

½ teaspoon sea salt

juice of 1 lemon

1 teaspoon fresh grated ginger

1 teaspoon grated garlic

½ teaspoon crushed red pepper flakes

spray of vegetable oil

grated zest of 1 orange

2 tablespoons chopped cilantro

1 teaspoon mint, chopped

Combine the shrimp with the salt and lemon juice in a bowl, and leave for 20 minutes; this cleans the shrimp and starts the "cooking" process by marination.

Rinse and dry the shrimp, then mix with the ginger, garlic, and chili. Spray with oil, mixing the shrimp well to make sure that they are all evenly coated.

Heat a frying pan over high heat. Tip in the shrimp and cook for 1–2 minutes on each side until they've turned pink. Toss with the orange zest, cilantro, and mint, and serve immediately.

Per serving

242 cals	3.4g fiber
3.7g fat	1.8g salt
0.4g saturated fat	
16.9g sugar	**1g fat per 100g**

Roast onions with curried crab

My sort of food takes a little effort. So, with a little effort here, you end up with a creatively different main course.

Serves 4

4 large onions, unpeeled

2 teaspoons vegetable oil

1 hot red pepper, finely diced

1 tablespoon Thai red curry paste

1 tablespoon smooth mango chutney

8 oz (1 cup) cooked long-grain rice (⅓ cup raw)

6 oz fresh or canned white crabmeat, flaked

2 tablespoons fat-free Greek yogurt

1 tablespoon chopped cilantro

1 tablespoon lime juice

1 tablespoon nam pla (fish sauce)

Place the onions, unpeeled and uncut, in a deep saucepan of salted water. Bring to a boil, reduce the heat, then simmer for 15–20 minutes. Remove and set aside until cool enough to handle.

Peel the onions, and cut a very shallow section off the root end to create a flat base. Cut one-fifth off the top of each onion and, with a teaspoon or melon baller, scoop out the center of each onion leaving at least two layers of onion on the outside to create the casing.

Preheat the oven to 350°F.

Chop half the onion centers finely and place in an ovenproof frying pan with the oil. Cook gently for 6–8 minutes, then add the chile and curry paste, and cook until fragrant, about 2 minutes. Add the chutney and rice, and stir to combine. Remove from the heat, and stir in the crab, yogurt, cilantro, lime juice, and fish sauce.

Fill the onions with this mixture, and place the pan on a baking sheet in the oven and roast for 25–30 minutes until bubbling.

Serve with purple sprouting broccoli and new potatoes.

Fruit and fiber chicken

Per serving
404 cals   2.6g fiber
3.5g fat   1g salt
0.6g saturated fat
29.7g sugar   **1.2g fat per 100g**

As we're not allowed to eat chicken skin, the question arises as to how to stop the flesh going leathery without the skin's protection. We need a crust, but not just any crust; we need a crust with flavor, so here it is. Serve with new potatoes, mustard and your favorite green vegetable.

Serves 4

⅓ cup rolled oats

2 teaspoons very finely chopped rosemary

grated zest of 1 orange

3 tablespoons dried cranberries, finely chopped

½ cup (4 oz) fat-free Greek yogurt

2 teaspoons whole grain Dijon-style mustard

1 egg white, beaten

4 x 6 oz skinless, boneless chicken breasts

½ cup (2 oz) seasoned flour

spray of olive oil

FILLING:

8 dried apricots

orange juice, for soaking

2 tablespoons plump golden raisins

2 tablespoons dried cherries

2 tablespoons dried blueberries

Cut open each apricot to create a pocket, then cover with orange juice. Let the raisins, cherries, and blueberries soak in orange juice in another bowl. Leave all the fruit to soak for 1 hour.

Combine the rolled oats, rosemary, orange zest, and chopped cranberries in one bowl, and beat together the yogurt, mustard, and egg white in another.

Place the chicken breasts on a chopping board and make a deep incision through the side of each breast, leaving the ends intact so you create deep pockets.

Mix together the drained raisins, cherries, and blueberries and use to stuff the apricot pockets. Push two filled apricots into the deep cut of each chicken breast, also pushing in any leftover berries.

Carefully roll the chicken breasts in the seasoned flour, then in the yogurt mixture, making sure that the coating has stuck to the flour, then finally roll the chicken in the oat mixture. Refrigerate until ready to use.

Preheat the oven to 350°F.

Spray the chicken in a fine mist of olive oil, place on a rack over a baking sheet and bake in the oven for 35 minutes. Season and serve.

Chicken in a pot

Per serving

269 cals   4.7g fiber

5g fat   1.1g salt

1.2g saturated fat

11.5g sugar   **1g fat per 100g**

Now, I would love to pot roast a whole chicken and I could ask you to remove the skin before carving, but would you? The skin also produces quite a lot of liquid fat during the cooking process, which you would have to skim off. This is all starting to sound like too much hassle, so skinless thighs it will be; these retain their moisture more than breasts, but if you prefer to use chicken breasts, feel free to substitute one small breast for every two thighs.

Serves 6

2 onions, roughly chopped

2 carrots, peeled and roughly chopped

2 sticks of celery, cut thinly

1 head of garlic, halved horizontally

2 teaspoons olive oil

3 sprigs of thyme

3 bay leaves

14 oz canned chopped tomatoes

1¼ cups (10 fl oz) dry white wine

12 chicken thighs

1¼ cups (10 fl oz) chicken stock

9 oz fresh penne pasta

⅔ cup (4 oz) frozen green peas, defrosted

1 zucchini, cut into pea-sized dice

Preheat the oven to 350°F.

In an ovenproof casserole dish with a lid, cook the onion, carrot, celery, and garlic in the oil over medium heat for about 8–10 minutes, until the onion starts to soften.

Add the thyme, bay leaves, tomatoes, and wine and bring to a boil. Nestle the chicken thighs into the vegetables, and add enough stock to make sure that everything is covered. Cover with the lid, and cook in the oven for 40 minutes.

Remove the chicken thighs and keep warm, then place the casserole on the stove top over high heat. Add any remaining stock, and bring to a boil.

Add the fresh pasta, peas, and zucchini, and stir to combine. Cook for 3 minutes, stirring frequently. Return the chicken to the pot and warm through. Serve with some crusty bread.

Tip

If you don't have any fresh pasta, use dried, but extend the cooking time accordingly.

Chicken and shrimp risotto

Per serving

482 cals	2.3g fiber
8.6g fat	3.4g salt
2.1g saturated fat	
4.3g sugar	**1.3g fat per 100g**

Risotto is about the rice. Too often in non-Italian countries, there's a habit of putting in far too many other ingredients, making the finished dish very heavy. Once you've mastered the slow addition of liquid, you are at liberty to experiment with the content. Risotto is often finished off with butter and Parmesan, which are low-fat no-nos, hence the addition of yogurt toward the end.

Serves 4

25 fl oz chicken stock

25 fl oz water

1 tablespoon olive oil

1 onion, finely diced

2 garlic cloves, crushed to a paste with a little sea salt

4 sage leaves, finely chopped

1 stick celery, finely diced

4 skinless boneless chicken thighs, each cut in 3

2 scant cups (11 oz) Arborio rice

16 raw tiger shrimp

spray of olive oil

2/3 cup (4 oz) frozen green peas, defrosted

2 tablespoons fat-free Greek yogurt

2 tablespoons chopped parsley

In a large saucepan, heat together the stock and water until boiling, then reduce the heat, and keep it at a simmer.

In another large, nonstick saucepan, heat the oil, then cook the onion over medium heat for 8 minutes, before adding the garlic, sage, celery, and chicken. Cook for another 3 minutes, gently coloring the chicken.

Add the rice, stir to combine and cook for a couple of minutes until the rice turns opaque, and releases a nutty aroma.

Add one ladleful of hot stock, and stir constantly until most of the liquid has evaporated, then add another ladleful and repeat. The heat should be reasonably aggressive, hence the reason for stirring. Carry on in this way until the rice is tender, but still a bit al dente, about 18–20 minutes. You may well not need all the stock.

Towards the end of the risotto cooking time, heat a frying pan, spray the shrimp with some oil, and pan-fry over high heat until pink all over. Add to the risotto, along with the peas, yogurt, and parsley. Stir to combine, season, and serve in four warm bowls.

Tip

As the rice cooks, it releases starch into the liquid creating a creamy emulsion. Risotto should not be dry—it should be a little soupy.

Turkey chow mein

Per serving
440 cals   7.2g fiber
12.4g fat   4.3g salt
3.5g saturated fat
11.1g sugar   **2.3g fat per 100g**

If you want to get the children to eat more healthily, then I'm afraid you may have to pander to their tastes, but don't worry, because actually, made well, this dish appeals to everyone. In many ways it's better than having it at your local Chinese restaurant, where the odd sprinkle of MSG tends to slip in.

Serves 4

2 teaspoons sesame oil
2 onions, finely chopped
1 carrot, peeled and finely chopped
1 green bell pepper, seeded and cut in
   ½-inch dice
2 garlic cloves, finely chopped
1 medium red pepper, thinly sliced
11 oz lean ground turkey or chicken
1 tablespoon mild Indian curry paste
4 oz shiitake mushrooms, stalks removed
   and discarded, caps finely sliced
¾ cup (6 fl oz) chicken stock
6 tablespoons oyster sauce
2 tablespoons low-sodium soy sauce
1 lb fresh thin egg noodles
½ cup (3 oz) frozen green peas, defrosted
2 bok choy, shredded

Heat the oil in a large wok, add the onion, carrot, bell pepper, garlic, chile, and ground turkey and cook over medium heat until the meat is golden, about 10 minutes. Break up any lumps of meat with the back of a wooden spoon as it cooks.

Add the curry paste and mushrooms, and stir to combine, cooking for 2 minutes, before adding the stock, and oyster and soy sauces.

Cook until boiling, then fold in the noodles, peas, and bok choy and cook for 2 minutes. Check the seasoning, and serve really hot.

Tip

Ground pork or beef could also be substituted for the turkey.

An Italian lamb feast

Per serving

456 cals   5.6g fiber

10.6g fat   0.5g salt

3.5g saturated fat

12.2g sugar   **1.9g fat per 100g**

This dish is a great alternative to a Sunday roast, though there's none of your pink lamb here. This is falling-off-the-bone-style cooking, which involves a little work towards the end of the cooking time, skimming off the fat, but is full of flavor.

Serves 6

1 small leg of lamb on the bone
(ideally no bigger than 2¼ lb)

2 garlic cloves, half sliced and half
finely chopped

½ bunch of fresh oregano or marjoram

2 onions, finely chopped

2 teaspoons olive oil

½ butternut squash, peeled, seeded
and cut into 1½-inch pieces

14 oz canned cherry tomatoes

14 oz canned chopped tomatoes

1 tablespoon Greek or wild dried
oregano

3 cups (12 oz) dried macaroni

1 tablespoon Lilliput (baby) capers,
drained

2 tablespoons chopped parsley

Preheat the oven to 300°F.

Make several slashes or deep holes all over the lamb, and insert a slice of garlic and a small sprig of oregano or marjoram into each cut. Season with salt and ground black pepper.

Place the onion, oil, and butternut squash in a bowl and toss together, then place in a roasting pan big enough to take the lamb. Pour in the two types of tomatoes, and the dried oregano, and stir to combine.

Place the lamb on top, and cook for 2½ hours. Pour a glass of water in every so often as the liquids in the pan dry out, and baste the lamb with the juices.

After the allotted time, remove the lamb to rest and keep warm, then pour the remains of the pan into a heatproof glass measuring cup and leave to stand for 5 minutes to allow the fat to separate from the juice. Skim off the fat, then tip the contents of the cup back into a saucepan and keep hot.

In another large saucepan, add enough boiling water to provide sufficient liquid to cook the pasta, then add the macaroni. Cook for 1 minute longer than suggested in the manufacturer's instructions. Drain the pasta, fold in the capers and parsley, and season to taste. Combine the cooked pasta and sauce, put the lamb back into the roasting pan, pour over the pasta and sauce, divide into portions, and serve.

Tip

Any leftovers will make for a delicious meal later in the week, when the flavors have intensified over time.

Turkey, spinach, and zucchini lasagna

Per serving	
382 cals	5.4g fiber
7.7g fat	1.5g salt
1.9g saturated fat	
14.8g sugar	**1.3g fat per 100g**

Everybody seems to enjoy lasagna but classically it's very high in fat, so I've reduced this by using less cheese and making a white sauce with cornstarch instead of the normal roux made with butter and flour.

Serves 6–8

2 scant cups (15 fl oz) skim milk

1 onion, halved

2 bay leaves

1 stick of celery

½ teaspoon ground nutmeg

1½ tablespoons cornstarch, loosened
  to a paste with a little water

11 oz frozen chopped spinach,
  defrosted

8 oz turkey cutlets, beaten thinly

8 green lasagna noodles

2 zucchini, thinly sliced lengthwise

½ cup (4 oz) low-fat cottage cheese

2 tablespoons grated Parmesan

SAUCE:

1 onion, finely chopped

1 tablespoon olive oil

2 garlic cloves, crushed to a paste
  with a little sea salt

2 anchovy fillets, roughly chopped

1 teaspoon dried oregano

12 pitted Kalamata black olives,
  roughly chopped

14 oz canned chopped tomatoes

2 teaspoons tomato paste

Preheat the oven to 400°F.

To make the tomato sauce, cook the onion in a large saucepan with the oil over medium to low heat for 8–10 minutes until softened, but not colored. Add the garlic, anchovy, and oregano, and cook for another 4 minutes until the anchovy breaks down. Add the olives, tomatoes, and tomato paste, and cook for 15 minutes until thick. Season and set aside.

Meanwhile, put the milk in a pan with the onion, bay leaves, celery, and nutmeg, and bring to a boil. Simmer for 15 minutes to infuse the flavors, then strain and return to a boil. Stir in the cornstarch paste, cook for 2–3 minutes to thicken, and check the seasoning.

Squeeze the spinach as dry as possible, then mix it with about a third of the white sauce. Spoon half the spinach mixture into the base of an ovenproof baking dish. Lay the turkey cutlets over the spinach, then spoon half the tomato sauce over the turkey. Lay on four lasagna noodles, then top with the remaining spinach. Next lay on the zucchini slices, and another four lasagna noodles followed by the remaining tomato sauce.

Pour over the white sauce, mixing it a little with the tomato sauce. Dot over the cottage cheese then sprinkle with Parmesan.

Bake in the oven for 45 minutes from cold, or 30 minutes if you're doing it immediately after putting it together.

Turkey ragù

Per serving

309 cals 2.9g fiber

10.3g fat 1.4g salt

4.1g saturated fat

10.2g sugar **2.5g fat per 100g**

A good ragù or Bolognese sauce is a useful standby for freezing, as you can use it for pasta, as a filling for shepherd's pie, or as a base for a moussaka or (cheese-free) lasagna. The chicken liver is barely noticeable when the meat has finished cooking, but it adds a great depth of flavor.

Serves 6

1 tablespoon olive oil

2 onions, finely diced

3 garlic cloves, crushed to a paste
  with a little sea salt

1 stick of celery, finely sliced

2 carrots, peeled and diced

2 bay leaves

2 tablespoons dried oregano

½ teaspoon crushed red chilli flakes

1½ lb ground turkey or chicken

6 oz chicken livers, chopped (optional)

¾ cup (6 fl oz) red wine

14 oz canned chopped tomatoes

1¼ cups (10 fl oz) chicken stock

1 tablespoon Worcestershire sauce

Put half the olive oil in a large saucepan, followed by the onions, garlic, celery, carrots, bay leaves, oregano, and chili, and cook for 8–10 minutes over medium heat, stirring frequently.

Add the remaining oil to a large frying pan, and, over high heat, cook the turkey and chicken livers, if using, until golden brown, breaking up any lumps with the back of a wooden spoon. Add to the vegetables.

Pour the wine into the empty frying pan and bring to a boil, scraping up any caramelized residue that has stuck to the bottom. Add to the ragù mixture.

Finally, add the chopped tomatoes, stock, and Worcestershire sauce, and bring to a boil, stirring frequently. Reduce the heat and simmer, covered, for at least 1½ hours. For the last 20 minutes, remove the lid to allow the mixture to thicken and reduce. Season and serve with pasta, rice, or any of the suggestions above.

Tip

If you allow the mixture to cool and then refrigerate it, you can then scoop off any fat that is sitting on the surface.

Asian bass in a bag

Per serving

257 cals	2.8g fiber
5.6g fat	0.9g salt
1g saturated fat	
2.3g sugar	**1.9g fat per 100g**

Cooking *"en papillote"*—the French name for this form of cookery—has slipped out of fashion for no particular reason other than laziness, and yet it is so simple, and seals in so much flavor.

Serves 4

1 teaspoon sesame oil

4 x 6 oz fillets of sea bass, scaled and pin-boned

1 teaspoon fresh grated ginger

½ teaspoon grated garlic

1 medium-heat red chili, seeded and sliced

4 scallions, thinly sliced on the diagonal

14 oz canned lima beans, drained and rinsed

1½ tablespoons low-sodium soy sauce

2 tablespoons sake, mirin, or dry sherry

8 cherry tomatoes, halved

Preheat the oven to 400°F.

Rub the sesame oil over the sea bass fillets, top and bottom, then lay each one, skin-side down, on a large rectangle of foil or baking parchment.

Combine the ginger, garlic, chili, and half the scallions, and sprinkle over the fish, then scatter around the lima beans.

Gather up the foil sides a little but before you seal the packages, pour in the soy sauce and sake, and top with the cherry tomatoes. Seal the packages tightly, and place on a baking sheet, then cook for 15 minutes.

Remove from the oven and allow to sit for 5 minutes. Open the package slightly and scatter with the remaining scallion slices.

Penne puttanesca

Per serving

447 cals	6.6g fiber
6.9g fat	2.3g salt
1g saturated fat	
8.7g sugar	**1.2g fat per 100g**

I've added extra chile to this classic pasta dish, but feel free to omit or increase the heat, and I've also had to drastically reduce the amount of oil. But please don't swamp your pasta with sauce: the Italians use just a little sauce to coat the pasta.

Serves 4

3 garlic cloves, finely chopped

4 anchovy fillets, drained and patted dry

2 tablespoons Lilliput (baby) capers

2 teaspoons extra-virgin olive oil

4 dried chiles, left whole

2 onions, finely chopped

1 teaspoon dried oregano

14 oz canned chopped tomatoes

½ cup (3 oz) Kalamata olives, pitted and chopped

½ cup (4 fl oz) water

14 oz dried penne

Bring a deep pan of heavily salted water to boil for the pasta.

In a large saucepan, cook the garlic, anchovies, and capers gently in the oil until the anchovies have broken down.

Add the chiles, onions, and oregano and cook gently for 8 minutes, then add the tomatoes, olives, and water. Bring to a boil, reduce the heat, and simmer until the sauce is dark and thick. Keep tasting the sauce as it cooks and, when it reaches the desired degree of chili heat, fish out the chiles.

Toward the end of the cooking time, boil the penne for about 1 minute less than it says on the manufacturer's instructions. Drain, and with the water still clinging to it, tip the pasta immediately into the sauce. Stir to combine, and serve immediately.

Aromatic vegetable packets

Per serving

110 cals   4.7g fiber

0.7g fat   0.5g salt

0.1g saturated fat

12.9g sugar   **0.2g fat per 100g**

When you're on one diet or another, it's vital to add a little inspiration to what will often be a dull menu. This dish is an exciting way to serve a lovely combination of different vegetables.

Serves 4

½ butternut squash, seeded and cut into ¾-inch chunks

2 celery hearts, cut in 4 lengthwise and washed thoroughly

1 red bell pepper, seeded and cut into strips

4 cocktail or pickling onions

4 radishes, trimmed

4 whole baby zucchini

2 teaspoons chopped mint

juice and grated zest of 1 orange

½ cup (4 fl oz) dry vermouth

½ teaspoon sweet paprika

¼ teaspoon sea salt

½ teaspoon freshly ground black pepper

Put all the vegetables in one bowl. Combine all the remaining ingredients in a separate bowl and stir well to incorporate.

Preheat the oven to 350°F, unless you prefer to use a steamer (see below).

Place four large squares of baking parchment (12 x 12 inch) on your work surface, and divide the vegetables between the four sheets. Working with one sheet at a time, bring the sides of the parchment up together to create an open package, then pour in a quarter of the aromatic liquid. Twist the paper edges together to seal the packel. Repeat with the others.

Either cook the packets in the oven for 35 minutes, or steam for 25 minutes, until the vegetables are tender.

Tip

You can obviously use different vegetables, but try to choose vegetables that will take the same time to cook. The citrus juices can be changed to lime and lemon, and the mint to cilantro or tarragon.

Beef pancakes with chili and ginger

Per serving

429 cals	2.9g fiber
11.5g fat	1g salt
5.2g saturated fat	
14.9g sugar	**3g fat per 100g**

We can get away with using beef by using less of it, and trimming off visible fat. With the addition of noodles and vegetables, we can eat this beef pancake with relish.

Serves 4

2 tablespoons ginger syrup (from the stem ginger below)

2 teaspoons low-sodium soy sauce

2 teaspoons dark brown sugar

1 teaspoon fresh grated ginger

2 garlic cloves, crushed to a paste with a little sea salt

1 hot red pepper, finely chopped

10 oz fillet steak, cut into thin strips

4 oz vermicelli (thin rice noodles)

spray of vegetable oil

1 leek, washed and cut into thin strips

1 carrot, peeled and cut into thin strips

4 store-bought Chinese pancakes

¼ pineapple, peeled and cored and cut into thin strips

1 tablespoon chopped cilantro

3 scallions, thinly sliced

1 ball stem ginger, cut into thin strips

In a bowl, combine the ginger syrup with the soy sauce, brown sugar, grated ginger, garlic, and red pepper. Stir to combine. Place the beef in a shallow dish, pour the marinade over, and leave to marinate for 2 hours.

Prepare the noodles by soaking them in hot water for 3 minutes, then refresh and drain them.

Spray a frying pan with vegetable oil, and place over high heat. Cook the marinated steak for 2 minutes, remove, and set aside to keep warm.

To the same pan, add the leek, carrot, and noodles, together with the marinade, and cook for 2 minutes to heat through.

Warm the pancakes in the microwave, then lay out on your work surface. Cover the surface of each pancake with the thin pineapple slices, then lay the beef down the center. Top the beef with the noodle mixture, followed by a sprinkling of cilantro, scallions, and stem ginger. Roll up and serve immediately.

Tip

This recipe works equally well with strips of chicken breast, or diced salmon or tuna.

Salads and side orders

Fennel, ruby grapefruit, and red onion salad

Per serving

55 cals 　　 2.3g fiber

3.7g fat 　　 0.5g salt

0.5g saturated fat

4.5g sugar 　　 **3g fat per 100g**

A classic combo that is a good source of folic acid and vitamin C. These lovely wintery flavors enhance broiled fish beautifully, and I can also see it going well with a roast chicken.

Serves 4

1 large fennel bulb, outside layer removed, very thinly sliced

1 ruby grapefruit, peeled, pith removed and segments cut from between each membrane, juices squeezed into a bowl

6 leaves from 1 Belgian endive, finely sliced

1 small red onion, finely sliced

½ teaspoon ground cumin

1 tablespoon extra-virgin olive oil

6 mint leaves, finely shredded

8 Kalamata olives in brine, pitted, rinsed, and drained

sea salt and ground black pepper

Add all the ingredients to the grapefruit juice and toss to combine. Season to taste.

Tip

If you find the salad too bitter, add one teaspoon of honey to the grapefruit juice before adding the remaining ingredients.

Fennel, apple, and red onion salad

Per serving

60 cals 　　 1.6g fiber

0.7g fat 　　 0.2g salt

0g saturated fat

8.8g sugar 　　 **0.5g fat per 100g**

A light, refreshing salad that would go well with fish.

Serves 4

2 tablespoons cider vinegar

4 tablespoons fat-free Greek yogurt

2 teaspoons Dijon mustard

1 teaspoon brown mustard seeds, soaked in cold water for 1 hour

1 teaspoon honey

1 Granny Smith apple, quartered, cored and thinly sliced

1 red onion, thinly sliced

1 small fennel bulb, outside layer removed, very thinly sliced

1 tablespoon chopped dill

Place the first five ingredients in a bowl and whisk to combine.

　　Mix the apple, onion, fennel, and dill then add enough dressing to coat. Season well.

Per serving

191 cals	2.8g fiber
4.4g fat	2.2g salt
1.1g saturated fat	
8.8g sugar	**1.3g fat per 100g**

Chili chicken salad

This is a salad you can make with the leftover Sunday roast chicken, but you could use cooked chicken breast, or poach a couple of chicken breasts to order, too.

Serves 4

11 oz cooked skinless chicken, shredded

1 carrot, peeled and cut into ribbons
   (use the peeler)

½ cucumber, peeled and cut into ribbons,
   discarding the seeds

4 radishes, thinly sliced

1 small red bell pepper, cut into strips

½ napa cabbage, thinly shredded

4 scallions, thinly sliced on the diagonal

¼ cup bean sprouts, soaked in ice water

1 red chili, seeded and thinly sliced

2 tablespoons cilantro leaves

2 handfuls of arugula leaves

CHILI DRESSING:

juice of 2 limes and grated zest of 1 lime

3 tablespoons sweet chili sauce

1 garlic clove, crushed to a paste with
   a little sea salt

½ teaspoon fresh grated ginger

1 tablespoon oyster sauce

1 teaspoon kecap manis (Indonesian soy
   sauce)

1 teaspoon sesame oil

Combine all the dressing ingredients in a bottle or jam jar, and shake well to mix. Leave for 30 minutes for the flavors to develop.

In a bowl, mix together all the salad ingredients, and coat with the dressing just before serving.

Panzanella—Italian bread and tomato salad

Per serving

154 cals   2g fiber

4.5g fat   1g salt

0.7g saturated fat

5.9g sugar   **2.9g fat per 100g**

Lycopene, vitamin C, and beta-carotene are all present here, which makes this healthy salad check all the right boxes when it comes to your well-being. I've reduced the oil, upped the vinegar, and softened it with a little sugar.

Serves 4

1 tablespoon extra-virgin olive oil

2 tablespoons red wine vinegar

½ teaspoon Tabasco sauce

2 garlic cloves, crushed to a paste
    with a little sea salt

3 tablespoons tomato juice or paste

1 teaspoon superfine sugar

1 small red onion, thinly sliced

3 beefsteak tomatoes, cored and cut
    into rough small chunks

3 thick slices day-old ciabatta bread,
    broken into rough chunks

10 large basil leaves, torn

Combine the oil with the vinegar, Tabasco, garlic, tomato juice, and sugar; stir to dissolve the sugar.

Add the onion, tomato, and bread, and stir to combine, check the seasoning, then scatter with basil. Allow the flavors to develop for 45 minutes before serving at room temperature.

Tip

If you prefer a softer texture to your bread, soak the chunks in cold water for 5 minutes, then squeeze to partially dry before adding to the salad. For a more crunchy salad, toast the bread before tearing it up, and adding to the salad.

Per serving

23 cals   1.1g fiber

0.2g fat   0g salt

0.1g saturated fat

4.4g sugar   **0.2g fat per 100g**

A tropical savory salad

This salad is based on the Indian "kachumber"—fresh, vibrant and healthy, with lots of zing.

Serves 6

¼ cucumber, peeled, seeded and
    cut into ½-inch chunks

1 small red onion, finely sliced

6 radishes, sliced

½ mango, peeled and cut into
    ½-inch chunks

3 tomatoes, seeded and cut
    into ½-inch dice

½ teaspoon superfine sugar

1 tablespoon chopped cilantro

2 teaspoons chopped mint

juice and grated zest of 1 lime

Combine all of the ingredients and serve immediately.

Tip

If you're going to prepare the salad ahead, add the herbs and lime juice just before serving.

Pomelo and pomegranate salad

Per serving

85 cals   2g fiber

0.6g fat   0.3g salt

0.1g saturated fat

17.4g sugar   **0.3g fat per 100g**

Sometimes you see pomelos in farmers' markets. In Thailand they separate all the juice droplets and make a fab salad, but that's fairly heavy-duty stuff, so all I'm asking here is for you to cut the fruit into segments. I've moved from Thailand to further West for my influences in this dish.

Serves 4

2 large pomelos

1 red onion, finely sliced

4 scallions, sliced

2 tablespoons chopped cilantro

1 teaspoon chopped mint

¼ small white cabbage, cored and finely shredded

2 garlic cloves, crushed to a paste with a little sea salt

1 teaspoon rose harissa

2 teaspoons honey

1 tablespoon pomegranate molasses

3 tablespoons pomegranate seeds

Peel the pomelos, remove the pith, and cut between the membranes to create segments. Do this over a bowl to catch the juices, then after segmenting, squeeze the empty membrane to release the remaining juice. Then separate the juice from the segments.

Combine the segments with the red onions, scallions, cilantro, mint, and cabbage in one bowl.

In the bowl containing the pomelo juice, add the garlic, harissa, honey, and pomegranate molasses. Mix to combine, then pour over the pomelo salad. Stir to mix well, then season before sprinkling over the pomegranate seeds. Serve immediately.

Tip

If pomelos are unobtainable, use a combination of red grapefruit and mandarin slices, peeled of course.

Pea, corn, and baby zucchini salad

Per serving

86 cals   2.7g fiber

2.1g fat   0.8g salt

0.4g saturated fat

8.3g sugar   **1.2g fat per 100g**

This is a really nice mixture that doubles up as a great vegetarian garnish. The miso paste adds a lovely nutty flavor.

Serves 4

1 teaspoon vegetable oil

3 scallions, sliced

2 red peppers, seeded and thinly sliced

11 oz canned corn kernels, drained

4 baby zucchini, halved lengthwise

²⁄₃ cup (4 oz) frozen green peas, defrosted

6 cherry tomatoes, halved

1 tablespoon low-sodium soy sauce

1 tablespoon light miso paste

juice of 1 lime

2 teaspoons chopped cilantro

Heat the oil in a frying pan, then add the scallions, chiles, corn kernels, zucchini, and peas, and cook for 2 minutes, stirring frequently. Add the tomatoes, soy sauce, and miso and stir until the miso combines with the other ingredients. Fold in the lime juice and cilantro, and check the seasoning.

Serve at room temperature as a salad, or hot as a vegetable.

Peperonata

Per serving

113 cals   3.9g fiber
3.5g fat   0.5g salt
0.5g saturated fat
12.9g sugar   **1.1g fat per 100g**

This is a lovely, vibrant summery dish which can be served as a salad, side order, or as part of an antipasti buffet. Bell peppers are a good source of beta-carotene, which helps to keep the carcinogenic free radicals at bay. This is really delicious folded into scrambled eggs.

Serves 4

2 red bell peppers, broiled, skinned and
    seeded, then cut in thin strips
1 yellow bell pepper, broiled, skinned and
    seeded, then cut in thin strips
1 green bell pepper, broiled, skinned and
    seeded, then cut in thin strips
1 tablespoon olive oil
1 red onion, thinly sliced
1 sprig thyme, leaves stripped
2 bay leaves
4 garlic cloves, crushed to a paste with
    a little sea salt
3 fl oz dry white wine
14 oz canned chopped tomatoes
8 basil leaves torn
sea salt and ground black pepper

Combine all the bell peppers with any cooking juices. In a frying pan heat the olive oil, then add the onion, and cook gently for 10–12 minutes to soften without color.

Add the thyme, bay leaves, and garlic, and cook for 3 minutes before increasing the temperature and adding the wine. Boil fast until almost all the liquid has evaporated. Add the cooked peppers and the tomato, and reduce the temperature, cook gently for 20–35 minutes, stirring from time to time until thick, and all the flavors have melded together. Stir in the basil and season to taste.

Tip

From time to time I like to intensify the flavors by adding some crushed red pepper flakes and chopped anchovy.

Indian roast potatoes

Per serving

266 cals   4.2g fiber

2.7g fat   0.1g salt

0.5g saturated fat

9.5g sugar   **0.7g fat per 100g**

So many interesting potato dishes involve the use of fat, whether it's butter, oil, or dripping. What I've tried to do here is provide a low-fat potato dish that can partner your meat or fish.

Serves 4

20 new potatoes, unpeeled, each cut
    into 4 wedges

2 teaspoons vegetable oil

4 large red peppers, each cut into
    four, lengthwise

8 garlic cloves, skin on, lightly crushed

2 red onions, each cut into 6 wedges

1 teaspoon ground cumin

½ teaspoon ground coriander

½ teaspoon ground turmeric

¼ teaspoon chili powder

½ teaspoon garam masala

1 teaspoon superfine sugar

juice of 1 lime

handful of cilantro leaves

Preheat the oven to 375°F.

Place the potatoes in a bowl and toss with the vegetable oil. Add the remaining ingredients, except the lime juice and cilantro leaves, and toss really thoroughly to ensure that all the vegetables are well covered with spices.

Tip into a baking pan and roast in the oven for 45–50 minutes, shuffling the vegetables around every few minutes to make sure none are burning.

When the potatoes are cooked, remove from the oven, and add the lime juice and cilantro leaves, tossing until the leaves wilt.

Stock-soaked spuds

Per serving

175 cals   3.8g fiber

1g fat   1.5g salt

0.2g saturated fat

8g sugar   **0.3g fat per 100g**

I used to be such a fan of dauphinoise potatoes, but that cream—delicious as it was—did none of us any favors. Here, I'm getting brilliant flavor but it's goodbye to all that fat.

Serves 6

2¼ lb russet potatoes, washed, skin on,
    very thinly sliced

2 large onions, thinly sliced

8 garlic cloves, peeled and thinly sliced

1 teaspoon chopped thyme leaves

6 bay leaves

spray of olive oil

1 orange, unpeeled, thinly sliced

lots of black pepper

2½ cups (20 fl oz) good vegetable or
    chicken stock

Preheat the oven to 375°F.

Combine the potato slices, onions, garlic, thyme, and bay leaves in a bowl. Spray with oil, season and toss to combine.

Arrange half the potatoes in a lightly oiled baking pan, pushing them flat, then make a layer of orange slices on top, followed by the remaining potato mixture, seasoning each layer with black pepper. Try to make the top layer into an attractive arrangement.

Pour in the stock—it will probably come up to over half the depth of the potatoes. Spray the top layer with a little oil, then cover the pan with foil.

Place in the oven for 30 minutes, then remove the foil and return to the oven to continue cooking, and to brown the surface. This will take another 40 minutes.

Bacon beans with sage, rosemary, and fennel

Per serving

179 cals 6.9g fiber

4g fat 1g salt

1g saturated fat

7g sugar **1.4g fat per 100g**

Once you've tasted these beans, you may well forgo canned baked beans in tomato sauce. Beans provide you with all sorts of health benefits—they are a source of protein, carbohydrate, iron, and other minerals, and of course provide you with important fiber.

Serves 4

2 teaspoons olive oil

3 slices Canadian bacon, fat removed, cut into strips

1 red onion, finely sliced

½ teaspoon chopped sage

½ teaspoon fennel seeds

½ sprig of rosemary, leaves stripped and finely chopped

1 mild long red pepper, seeded and finely diced

28 oz canned white beans (cannellini, navy or lima), drained and rinsed

14 oz canned chopped tomatoes

1 teaspoon superfine sugar

2 tablespoons chopped parsley

Heat the olive oil in a large saucepan, then add the bacon pieces and cook until golden. Add the red onion, sage, fennel seeds, rosemary, and chile to the pan, and cook over medium heat for 8–10 minutes without coloring the onion too much.

Add the beans and tomatoes, and cook gently until the sauce is thick, about 12–15 minutes, then fold in the sugar and parsley. Season to taste.

Tip

The beans taste great served on whole wheat toast, or as a partner to broiled meat or fish. Vegetarians can, of course, enjoy them without the bacon.

Asian greens in black bean sauce

Per serving

91 cals 3.8g fiber

3.6g fat 1.5g salt

0.6g saturated fat

5.6g sugar **1.3g fat per 100g**

I can't get enough of Chinese greens. I haven't persuaded my children to get so excited about them, though they're slowly coming around. This is a great way to eat them, the perfect accompaniment for a plain piece of meat or fish.

Serves 4

2 teaspoons sesame oil

⅔ cup (4 oz) sugar snap peas, trimmed

9 oz Chinese broccoli

8 baby zucchini cut in half lengthwise

2 heads of bok choy cut in half lengthwise

1 teaspoon garlic paste

½ teaspoon ginger paste

1 medium-hot red pepper, seeded and chopped

3 fl oz vegetable stock

2 tablespoons black bean sauce

1 tablespoon kecap manis (Indonesian soy sauce)

1 teaspoon sesame seeds

Heat the oil in a wok, then add the sugar snap peas, broccoli, zucchini and bok choy, and stir-fry for 2 minutes. Add the garlic and ginger pastes, and the pepper, and stir to combine.

Pour in the stock, black bean sauce, and kecap manis and cook for 1 minute.

Transfer to a warm dish and serve sprinkled with sesame seeds.

Tip

Unless you've got a Chinese supermarket in your area, some of the greens may not be available, but you can always improvise with Western greens.

Green beans with cherry tomatoes

Per serving (based on 4 servings)	
60 cals	2.8g fiber
2.2g fat	0.3g salt
0.3g saturated fat	
5.8g sugar	**1.1g fat per 100g**

It's great to eat your vegetables, but it's even better to jazz them up with a little extra flavor, especially if they're accompanying a piece of steamed fish or grilled meat. You don't have to use beans, you can try any green vegetable.

Serves 4–6

12 oz extra fine green beans, trimmed

2 teaspoons olive oil

½ onion, finely chopped

2 garlic cloves, finely sliced

2 anchovy fillets in oil, drained and patted dry with paper towels

1 hot red pepper, left whole

14 oz canned cherry tomatoes

8 basil leaves, torn

Bring a pan of salted water to a boil and cook the beans for 3–4 minutes, leaving a little bite. Drain.

Meanwhile, heat the olive oil in a frying pan, and cook the onion over medium heat for 8 minutes. Add the garlic, anchovies, and chile and cook for 3–4 minutes more, until the anchovies start to break down.

Add the tomatoes, and bring to a boil, season, then add the beans and basil. Warm through, season and serve.

Per serving (based on 6 servings)	
110 cals	3.2g fiber
2.2g fat	0.3g salt
0.4g saturated fat	
7.6g sugar	**0.7g fat per 100g**

Fattoush with tomato dressing

This Middle Eastern salad is a mixture of fresh vibrant color, the crunch of raw vegetables, and baked pita. I've replaced much of the olive oil with puréed tomatoes.

Serves 4–6

7 ripe tomatoes, roughly chopped

2 garlic cloves, roughly chopped

juice of 2 lemons

2 teaspoons extra-virgin olive oil

2 handfuls of arugula leaves

1 tablespoon ground sumac

2 pita breads

1 cucumber, peeled, cut in half lengthwise, seeded and chopped

1 red onion, thinly sliced

4 scallions, thinly sliced on the diagonal

6 radishes, thinly sliced

handful of flat-leaf parsley

12 mint leaves, shredded

2 Baby Gem lettuces, leaves separated

Preheat the oven to 350°F.

In a food processor, blend half the tomatoes with the garlic, lemon juice, olive oil, half the arugula leaves, and the sumac until smooth. Season with salt and pepper and set aside.

Split the pita bread in half then break into irregular pieces. Place on a rack in the oven and bake for about 15 minutes, until crisp and brittle, then remove and set aside to cool.

In a bowl, combine the remaining tomatoes, cucumber, red onion, scallions, radishes, parsley, mint, and lettuce.

Just before serving, dress the salad with the tomato dressing and scatter with the crisp pita pieces.

Asian pork and lychee salad

Per serving

155 cals   2.2g fiber

3g fat   0.9g salt

0.1g saturated fat

16.9g sugar   **1.3g fat per 100g**

Ever since I was a boy I have loved canned lychees even more than the fresh ones, which appear to be picked before the sugars have developed. Pork is one of our lowest-fat meats, and I tend to cook it with a hint of mint to retain its juiciness. It's your call, but I can tell you that pork is safe to eat even when it is a little pink.

Serves 4

spray of vegetable oil

9 oz pork tenderloin, any visible fat removed

12 canned lychees, drained

½ red bell pepper, seeded and cut into thin strips

½ yellow bell pepper, seeded and cut into thin strips

1 Asian pear, cored and cut into strips or thin crescents, seeds removed

zest of 2 limes

¾-inch piece of fresh ginger, peeled and cut into thin strips

1 cup (2 oz) watercress, large stems discarded

12 mint leaves, shredded

6 basil leaves, shredded

4 scallions, thinly sliced on the diagonal

2 tablespoons bean sprouts, soaked in ice water

1 tablespoon pink pickled ginger, drained and cut into thin strips

DRESSING:

lime juice from the 2 limes (above)

1 teaspoon finely chopped garlic

1 bird's eye chile, very thinly shredded

1 tablespoon pickled ginger juice

1 tablespoon rice vinegar

1 tablespoon nam pla (fish sauce)

2 teaspoons honey

Spray a nonstick frying pan with oil and place over medium heat. Add the pork, brown all over, and cook until done to your liking, about 10 minutes. Remove and allow to cool.

Combine all the ingredients for the dressing, stirring to combine.

Slice the pork thinly, and add to the dressing, tossing to combine. Allow to stand for 15 minutes.

Toss together all the remaining salad ingredients, so everything is evenly distributed, then add the pork slices and dressing. Toss again, and serve immediately.

Tip

This recipe works equally well with cooked chicken breast. If you can't find Asian pears just use concorde or anjou.

Crab and grapefruit salad

Per serving

154 cals   2g fiber

5.2g fat   3g salt

0.7g saturated fat

7.9g sugar   **1.8g fat per 100g**

There's nothing nicer than fresh crab. However, if you're like me, you don't enjoy picking out the flesh from the shell. In good fish markets, you can usually find freshly picked crabmeat, which has often been pasteurized first, but tastes good. If not, *avoid* the frozen kind and go instead for canned crab in brine, which is pretty good.

Serves 4–6

¼ napa cabbage (5 oz),
     very thinly shredded

½ cucumber, seeded and cut into
     ½-inch dice

2 ripe tomatoes, seeded and diced

12 mint leaves, shredded

1 ruby grapefruit, skinned, pith
     removed, and segments cut from
     between the membranes

4 scallions, thinly sliced on
     the diagonal

12 oz fresh or canned crabmeat,
     drained and picked over for
     rogue pieces of shell

DRESSING:

juice from membranes of the grapefruit

1 garlic clove, crushed to a paste with a
     little sea salt

2 teaspoons sweet chili sauce

1 teaspoon fresh grated ginger

2 tablespoons nam pla (fish sauce)

1 teaspoon superfine sugar

2 bird's eye chiles, finely chopped

For the dressing, simply place all the ingredients in a clean jam jar, put the lid on, and shake.

Combine all the salad ingredients, and add enough dressing to coat. Toss well and serve.

Tip

When segmenting a grapefruit, cut between the membranes holding the peeled grapefruit over a bowl to catch any juices, then squeeze out any juices from the core and the membranes.

A different green salad

Per serving
108 cals   4.1g fiber
4.7g fat   1.1g salt
0.7g saturated fat
4g sugar   **3g fat per 100g**

This chunky legume salad with the vibrant colors of spring greens is designed for texture, taste and health.

Serves 4

1 teaspoon fresh grated ginger

2 garlic cloves, crushed to a paste
    with a little sea salt

1 red pepper, finely sliced

2 teaspoons vegetable or peanut oil

1 teaspoon mustard seeds

4 scallions, thinly sliced on
    the diagonal

juice of 2 lemons

1 tablespoon nam pla (fish sauce)

1 teaspoon superfine sugar

4 oz extra fine green beans, trimmed
    and cut into ¾-inch pieces

generous cup (7 oz) frozen green peas,
    defrosted

6 oz frozen podded edamame beans,
    defrosted

12 mint leaves, shredded

½ bunch of cilantro, roughly chopped

Make the dressing. Place the ginger, garlic, and red pepper in a pan with the oil and gently heat to release the flavor, rather than cook. Increase the heat, add the mustard seeds and cook until they're jumping. Turn off the heat, then add the scallions, lemon juice, nam pla, and sugar. Toss to combine, season, then set aside.

Meanwhile, heat a deep pan of salted water to boiling, then add the green beans and cook for 2 minutes. Add the peas and edamame beans, and cook for another minute.

Drain the vegetables and add to the dressing in the other pan. Add the herbs, and toss to combine. Serve cold, hot, or at room temperature.

Tip

Edamame beans, which are a soy bean and a good source of protein, are becoming more widely available, but if you can't find them substitute with frozen baby fava beans.

Cool and hot cucumber salad

Per serving
22 cals   0.9g fiber
0.2g fat   1.3g salt
0g saturated fat
3.4g sugar   **0.1g fat per 100g**

This salad makes a great accompaniment for grilled fish, such as salmon. It has a wonderful fresh taste.

Serves 4

1 large cucumber, thinly sliced

1 teaspoon salt

2 medium-heat, long green peppers,
    seeded and finely diced

1 red pepper, seeded and finely diced

1 tablespoon chopped cilantro

1 teaspoon chopped mint

2 tablespoons cider vinegar

½ teaspoon Tabasco sauce

1 teaspoon superfine sugar

Place the cucumber slices in a colander, sprinkle with the salt, and toss well. Place over a bowl or in the sink and allow the salt to extract the cucumber water for 20 minutes; then rinse under running water and pat dry.

Combine the remaining ingredients in a bowl, add the cucumber, and check the seasoning. Allow the flavors to develop for 20 minutes before serving.

Tip

If you want to keep the cucumber bright green, add the vinegar only just before serving.

Low-fat jeweled couscous

Per serving
420 cals   3.1g fiber
2.2g fat   0.9g salt
0.4g saturated fat
22.2g sugar   **0.8g fat per 100g**

Couscous is very bland in its natural state, but with my additions you've got yourself a great salad, or accompaniment to a tagine or stew.

Serves 6

1¼ cups (10 fl oz) chicken stock
1¼ cups (10 fl oz) water
1½ cups (9 oz) couscous
grated zest of 1 lemon
2 teaspoons extra-virgin olive oil
⅓ cup (2 oz) dried cherries
⅓ cup (2 oz) frozen green peas, defrosted
¾ cup (4 oz) dried apricots, chopped
⅓ cup (2 oz) golden raisins
1 zucchini, coarsely grated
2 heaping tablespoons chopped
   flat-leaf parsley
2 heaping tablespoons chopped cilantro

Heat the stock and water in a pan until boiling. Pour in the couscous in a thin, steady stream, then stir in the lemon zest. Cover with plastic wrap and set aside for 5 minutes to allow the grains to swell. Fluff up the grains with a fork so that they separate. (You can prepare ahead to this stage.)

Return the couscous to the heat and drizzle over the olive oil. Cook gently for a few minutes, stirring with a fork to fluff up the grains, then remove from the heat. Fold in the remaining ingredients, and season to taste. If not serving immediately, tip the couscous into an ovenproof dish, cover with foil and keep warm in the bottom of a medium-hot oven until you're ready to serve.

Roast carrot and beet salad with cottage cheese

Per serving
131 cals   3.8g fiber
3.8g fat   0.5g salt
0.8g saturated fat
15.7g sugar   **1.5g fat per 100g**

Roasting the carrots and beets caramelizes the edges and intensifies the sweetness of the vegetables. The choice of salad leaves must be yours, but I enjoy a bag of wild arugula and watercress.

Serves 4

16 baby beets, washed
1 tablespoon olive oil
2 bay leaves
6 sprigs of thyme
12 baby carrots, scrubbed, but left whole
8 garlic cloves, unpeeled
3 tablespoons sherry vinegar
2 teaspoons honey
1 bag of mixed salad leaves
½ cup (4 oz) low-fat cottage cheese

Preheat the oven to 400°F.

Toss the beets in the olive oil with the bay leaves and thyme. Place in a roasting pan, season, and roast for 45 minutes. Add the carrots and garlic, then return to the oven and cook for another 35 minutes.

Remove the beets and garlic, and, when cool enough to handle, squeeze them out of their skins. Return to the roasting pan, and toss all the vegetables with the vinegar and honey.

Arrange the salad leaves on four plates, and scatter over the vegetables and garlic with their juices. Crumble over the cottage cheese and serve.

Tip

If you can't find raw baby beets, buy cooked beets and add with the carrots or cut larger beets into small wedges, and follow the recipe above.

Winter vegetables in a pot

Per serving

196 cals	7.7g fiber
4.9g fat	0.2g salt
0.8g saturated fat	
15.2g sugar	**1.5g fat per 100g**

Forget the protein, I could eat a pot of these vegetables just as they are. I've chosen my favorite vegetables, but you can vary the mixture depending on your likes and dislikes.

Serves 4

2 onions, cut into 8 wedges

2 parsnips, peeled and quartered

12 Brussels sprouts, trimmed

8 carrots, trimmed

2 sticks of celery, each cut crosswise into 3

½ butternut squash, seeded, skin removed, and cut into manageable chunks

1 tablespoon chopped thyme

8 unpeeled garlic cloves

¾ cup (6 fl oz) dry vermouth or dry white wine

2 tablespoons extra-virgin olive oil

14 oz canned cannellini beans, drained and rinsed

¾ cup (6 fl oz) water

TO SERVE:

1 teaspoon finely chopped garlic

grated zest of 1 unwaxed lemon

3 tablespoons chopped parsley

2 tablespoons sherry vinegar

2 teaspoons honey

Put everything except the beans, water, and serving ingredients in an ovenproof, lidded pot and toss with the oil and some salt and pepper. Allow to sit for 30 minutes to allow the flavors to develop.

Preheat the oven to 425°F.

Cover the pot with a lid, place in the center of the oven, and cook the vegetables for 1 hour. After this time, fold in the cannellini beans along with the water, then return to the oven, uncovered, and cook for another 20 minutes.

Combine the serving ingredients, and just before you're ready to eat, stir them into the vegetables and check the seasoning.

Summer peas with bacon, lettuce, and mint

Per serving
115 cals   4.5g fiber
5.5g fat   1.6g salt
1.3g saturated fat
5.1g sugar   **2.4g fat per 100g**

This side dish is based on *"petits pois à la française"* a fabulous combination of flavors. Unless you grow your own, I would always recommend using frozen petits pois, because they usually have more vitamins than so-called "fresh," which may have been hanging around for a few days since being picked. If you can't find petits pois, use green peas instead.

Serves 4

1 tablespoon olive oil

4 scallions, finely sliced

3 slices Canadian bacon, fat removed, cut into strips

1 garlic clove, crushed to a paste with a little sea salt

2 Baby Gem lettuces, washed and shredded

11 oz frozen petits pois, defrosted

⅔ cup (5 fl oz) vegetable stock

1 teaspoon superfine sugar

2 teaspoons chopped mint

In a medium saucepan, heat the oil with the scallions and bacon, and cook gently for 4–6 minutes. Add the garlic and lettuce and cook, stirring frequently, for 5 minutes until the lettuce wilts.

Add the peas, stock, and sugar, increase the heat, and boil vigorously for 5 minutes. Fold in the mint and season; it shouldn't need much salt, but a few twists of pepper will add a nice dimension.

Per serving
67 cals   4.4g fiber
3.6g fat   0.2g salt
0.5g saturated fat
4.7g sugar   **1.8g fat per 100g**

Curried peas with mint and tomato

Peas are loved by almost everybody, but they can become repetitive, so here's a recipe to add a little variety.

Serves 4

2 teaspoons vegetable oil

2 teaspoons brown mustard seeds

1 teaspoon fresh grated ginger

4 scallions, finely sliced

1 red pepper, seeded and finely diced

1 teaspoon ground cumin

½ teaspoon ground coriander

¼ teaspoon ground fennel

½ teaspoon ground turmeric

3 tomatoes, roughly chopped

⅔ cup (5 fl oz) water

½ teaspoon garam masala

1 tablespoon chopped mint

1 teaspoon chopped cilantro

11 oz frozen green peas, defrosted

Heat the oil in a saucepan. Add the mustard seeds, wait until they start to pop, then add the ginger, scallions, chile, and ground spices. Cook for a minute, then add the tomatoes and water.

Bring everything to a boil, cook for 3 minutes, then add the garam masala, mint, cilantro, and peas and cook for 6 minutes. Check the seasoning and serve.

Smoked chicken and parsley salad

Per serving

283 cals

7g fat

1.2g saturated fat

3.9g sugar

4.3g fiber

1.7g salt

2g fat per 100g

The smokiness of the chicken breast contrasts nicely with the mild new potatoes, while the flat-leaf parsley leaves combined with the arugula and watercress add another dimension to the dish. And then there's that lovely hot/cold sensation.

Serves 4

1 lb red boiling potatoes, each cut lengthwise into 6 wedges

8 oz frozen edamame beans, defrosted

4 oz extra fine green beans

8 oz smoked chicken breasts, skinned and thinly sliced

4 scallions, thinly sliced

2 cups (2oz) arugula leaves

1 bunch of flat-leaf parsley, leaves picked, stalks retained

1 cup (2 oz) watercress, tough stems removed

HERB DRESSING:

parsley stalks from above, roughly chopped

1 tablespoon olive oil

4 tablespoons fat-free Greek yogurt

2 teaspoons Dijon mustard

1 sprig of tarragon, leaves only, finely chopped

1 tablespoon Lilliput (baby) capers, drained

4 gherkins, finely chopped

Heat a pan of salted water and cook the potatoes until tender, about 15 minutes. Add the edamame and green beans, and cook for another 4 minutes.

Meanwhile, make the dressing in a food processor: blend together the parsley stalks, olive oil, and yogurt with a little salt and pepper until smooth. Pass through a fine sieve into a bowl, and fold in the remaining ingredients. Mix well and check the seasoning.

When the potatoes and beans have cooked, drain and set aside. Combine the chicken breast with the scallions, arugula, parsley, and watercress. Fold in the warm vegetables, then add enough of the dressing to coat. Serve immediately.

Tip

Vary the potato variety to those grown in your area. The bulk of the salad can be made ahead, as can the dressing, but don't cook or add the vegetables until just before serving.

A potato salad with bite

Per serving
243 cals   4.2g fiber
1.1g fat   1.4g salt
0.1g saturated fat
8.2g sugar   **0.3g fat per 100g**

With all my potato salads, I like to dress them warm, so that the potatoes absorb the flavors, and I also like to slightly overcook old russet potatoes, so that their edges are starting to break up.

Serves 4

2¼ lb russet potatoes, peeled and
    cut into 1-inch dice
1 onion, finely chopped
2 tablespoons Lilliput (baby) capers,
    drained
4 anchovy fillets, drained and chopped
6 cornichons (baby gherkins),
    thinly sliced
2 sweet gherkins, cut into ¼-inch dice
4 tablespoons chopped parsley
2 tablespoons snipped chives
2 teaspoons chopped mint
½ teaspoon ground white pepper
5 tablespoons fat-free Greek yogurt

Cook the potatoes in salted water until tender, about 15–20 minutes. Drain well in the colander, tossing them around so that the edges break up a little.

Meanwhile, as the potatoes are cooking, combine the onion, capers, anchovies, cornichons, gherkins, herbs, and pepper in a bowl. Fold in the yogurt and season.

While the potatoes are still warm, add the herb dressing, and stir to combine. Serve the salad at room temperature.

Tip

For a better GI rating, you could use new potatoes, but the texture won't be the same.

An autumn orchard salad

Per serving
139 cals   2.4g fiber
5g fat   0.9g salt
2.9g saturated fat
15g sugar   **2.4g fat per 100g**

This is a great autumn salad when orchard fruits are at their best.

Serves 4

2 oz Roquefort cheese, crumbled
scant cup (7 oz) fat-free Greek yogurt
1 tablespoon snipped chives
½ teaspoon chopped tarragon
4 cornichons, thinly sliced
1 teaspoon Lilliput (baby) capers,
    drained
1 teaspoon lemon juice
1 teaspoon honey
1 dessert pear, halved, cored,
    then thinly sliced
2 crisp apples, halved, cored, then
    thinly sliced
1 bag washed watercress and arugula

Combine the Roquefort and yogurt and mash well to combine. Add the herbs, cornichons, capers, lemon juice, and honey, and season to taste.

Fold the fruit into the dressing and toss to combine.

Arrange the salad leaves on four plates, then scatter over the fruit mixture, arranging neatly if preferred.

Tip

You could throw in a few blackberries for added orchard flavors, in which case, change the tarragon to mint.

Roast cauliflower with beans and bok choy

Per serving

78 cals	3.8g fiber
1.6g fat	0.9g salt
0.3g saturated fat	
8.3g sugar	**0.6g fat per 100g**

Boiled cauliflower doesn't do it for me—it cries out for cheese sauce, but as we all know, that's not allowed to feature in our low-fat diet. Recently, however, I had roast cauliflower and was impressed; it adds a lovely nuttiness to the flavor, and the cauliflower retains a little crunch.

Serves 6

1 cauliflower (approx. 1½ lb), cut into bite-size florets, the central core discarded

1 onion, cut into 8 wedges

3 garlic cloves, crushed to a paste with a little sea salt

spray of vegetable oil

4 scallions, finely sliced on the diagonal

2 medium-heat chiles, finely sliced

4 tablespoons water or vegetable stock

6 oz extra fine green beans, trimmed and cut into 1-inch pieces

2 heads of bok choy, cut in quarters lengthwise

1 tablespoon chopped cilantro roots and stems (see Tip)

1 tablespoon low-sodium soy sauce

1 tablespoon oyster sauce

2 teaspoons honey

1 tablespoon cilantro leaves

Preheat the oven to 400°F.

Place the cauliflower in a bowl with the onion and garlic, and spray all over with the oil. Season with salt and ground black pepper, then place in a roasting pan in the oven and roast for 20 minutes, turning frequently. Remove and set aside.

Six minutes before the end of the roasting time, spray a wok with oil and, over high heat, stir-fry the scallions and chile for 1 minute. Add the water, and bring to a boil, then add the beans and cook for 3 minutes. Add the bok choy and cook for another minute.

Add the cilantro roots and stems, soy and oyster sauces, and honey, and stir-fry for 1 minute. Finally, add the hot cauliflower mixture and toss to combine. Sprinkle with cilantro leaves.

Tip

The Thais use cilantro roots and stems a lot in their cooking, but you might find it hard to find bunches with roots unless you use an Asian supermarket. Alternatively, just use finely chopped stems.

Purple sprouting broccoli with cannellini beans and spinach

Per serving

164 cals   10.2g fiber

2.6g fat   0.8g salt

0.5g saturated fat

5.5g sugar   **0.9g fat per 100g**

I'm not going to tell you how to cook your vegetables, but I will suggest how to jazz them up to make that plain bit of chicken or fish a little more exciting. If you like anchovies, you'll love this, and it would go perfectly with some roast cod.

Serves 4

1 red onion, cut into 8 wedges

spray of olive oil

4 garlic cloves, crushed to a paste
with a little sea salt

4 anchovy fillets, roughly chopped

pinch of dried oregano

pinch of crushed red pepper flakes

28 oz canned cannellini beans, rinsed
and drained

14 oz purple sprouting broccoli,
woody stems removed

2 handfuls of baby spinach leaves,
wet from washing

Put a deep pan of salted water on to boil.

Meanwhile, place the onion wedges in a nonstick saucepan, spray with oil, and cook over gentle heat for 12–15 minutes, to soften, but not color. Add the garlic, anchovies, oregano, and red pepper flakes, and toss to combine. Cook for 2 minutes until the anchovies break down. Add the beans to the onions, toss to combine, and season well.

While the onions are cooking, put the broccoli in the boiling water and cook for 6–8 minutes. I want the broccoli to be a bit softer than you would normally cook it, and absorb some water. Then, using a slotted spoon, scoop the broccoli from the pan, allowing some water to cling to it. Spoon into the beans and combine quite vigorously so that the broccoli heads break up, leaving the beans speckled with green.

Finally, fold in the spinach, and cook until wilted, about 2 minutes.

Tip

If purple sprouting broccoli is unavailable, feel free to substitute ordinary broccoli.

A Piedmontese-style pepper

Per serving

139 cals	3.5g fiber
6.5g fat	0.6g salt
3.8g saturated fat	
12.4g sugar	**2.4g fat per 100g**

This is a very popular appetizer at my pub, The Greyhound. We put it on the menu whenever my fruit and vegetables supplier sends peppers by the boxful at an attractive price! Delicious topped with a slice of low-fat mozzarella.

Serves 4

4 tomatoes, cored

4 red or yellow bell peppers, halved lengthwise through the stalk, seeded

3 garlic cloves, thinly sliced

16 basil leaves

4 anchovy fillets, each cut in 4

spray of olive oil

3½ oz low-fat mozzarella cheese, cut into 8 slices

Place the tomatoes in a bowl and pour over boiling water; leave for 1 minute, then plunge into cold water. Remove the skins, then halve the tomatoes.

Preheat the oven to 400°F.

In the bottom of each pepper, place a few slices of garlic, a couple of basil leaves and a couple of pieces of anchovy. Leave for 10 minutes.

Push half a tomato into each pepper cavity, squashing it in tightly so that it tucks in under the edge of the pepper and spray lightly with olive oil. Put into a roasting pan, ideally on a rack, and place in the oven. Cook for 20 minutes, then turn the oven down to 350°F, and cook for another 25 minutes. For the last 8–12 minutes of cooking, top each pepper with a slice of mozzarella and cook until melted.

Spiced cauliflower with red lentil sauce

Per serving

269 cals	6g fiber
6.1g fat	1.5g salt
0.9g saturated fat	
9.4g sugar	**1.5g fat per 100g**

This is a really "meaty" vegetarian dish that has lots of flavor and the crunch of undercooked cauliflower.

Serves 4

1 tablespoon vegetable oil

1 onion, finely chopped

3 garlic cloves, crushed to a paste with a little sea salt

2 tablespoons ground cumin

2 teaspoons ground coriander

1 cup (7 oz) red lentils, rinsed

1¼ cups (10 fl oz) vegetable stock

14 oz canned cherry tomatoes

1 small cauliflower, broken into small florets

spray of vegetable oil

2 teaspoons chopped cilantro

In a large saucepan, heat the vegetable oil and cook the onion and garlic gently for 8–10 minutes. Add half the spices and the lentils, and stir to combine.

Add the stock and cherry tomatoes, bring to a boil, then reduce the heat and simmer until the lentils start to break down, about 25 minutes.

Meanwhile, spray the cauliflower florets with vegetable oil, then dust with the remaining spices. Cook in a frying pan over high heat to brown the cauliflower all over, add to the lentils, and cook for 2 minutes.

Garnish with cilantro and serve with rice.

Desserts and cakes

Campari and orange sorbet

Per serving
170 cals
0g fat
0g saturated fat
40.6g sugar

0.1g fiber
0g salt

0g fat per 100g

A great palate cleanser that is perfect to finish a meal, it's light and cooling, and you're also getting loads of vitamin C, plus a smattering of potassium and beta-carotene which will help you fight off the winter chills.

Serves 4

juice of 6 oranges and the grated zest
　of 1 orange
½ cup (4 oz) superfine sugar
2 sprigs mint
3 tablespoons Campari

Heat the orange juice with the zest, sugar, and mint in a non-reactive saucepan until it comes to a boil and the sugar has dissolved. Allow to cool to room temperature, add the Campari, remove the mint and discard. Pour into your ice cream machine, and follow the manufacturer's instructions. Keep in the freezer.

This is best eaten on the day it is made, as homemade sorbets tend to go hard. If this happens, allow the sorbet to defrost, then re-churn.

Tip

If you don't have an ice-cream machine you'd be better off turning this recipe into a granita, which is a water ice. Simply pour the cooled mixture into a shallow tray and place in the freezer. After about 1 hour, when the mix is starting to freeze, break it up with a whisk and repeat every 15 minutes until you have a frozen slush.

Affogato—adult coffee and ice cream

Per serving
111 cals
3.1g fat
1.8g saturated fat
14.7g sugar

0g fiber
0.1g salt

2.4g fat per 100g

I rarely eat desserts, but I do love an after-dinner coffee. This simple dessert is an Italian classic that demands fresh coffee, which happens to be a good source of riboflavin, one of the B vitamins. Like most of your diet, coffee should be taken in sensible moderation.

Serves 4

4 scoops reduced-fat vanilla ice cream
4 freshly made double espressos
8 teaspoons coffee liqueur

Place 1 scoop of ice cream in 4 cappuccino cups or glass bowls.

Pour over the espresso, sweetened if required, then top off with coffee liqueur. Serve *immediately*.

Tip

You can mix and match the liqueur using brandy or whiskey instead of coffee liqueur.

Zabaglione-glazed raspberries

Per serving

117 cals	2.8g fiber
3.7g fat	0g salt
1.1g saturated fat	
16.8g sugar	**2.5g fat per 100g**

Zabaglione is a classic Italian recipe in its own right, of course, but it also makes a great topping for soft fruits. Here I'm using raspberries, but feel free to use whatever is in season. This recipe is the original "foam" conceived long before the penchant for foams became commonplace among modern young chefs.

Serves 4

2 pints (1 lb) fresh raspberries
2 egg yolks
2 tablespoons superfine sugar
2 tablespoons sweet sherry or Marsala
2 tablespoons orange juice

Arrange the raspberries in four shallow heatproof gratin dishes.

Combine the remaining ingredients in a bowl and set it over a saucepan of simmering water, making sure that the water doesn't touch the bottom of the bowl. With an electric whisk (or by hand if you're fit), whisk the mixture for 8–10 minutes, or until it's light, frothy, and holds its own shape. You will find that you want to stop after 2–3 minutes, but don't, because the eggs won't have "cooked" and the foam will collapse very quickly.

Preheat the broiler.

Spoon the foam over the raspberries, then broil until browned in patches. Beware, the color can change in an instant, and you could end up with delicious scrambled egg!

Roast peaches with amaretti and raspberries

Per serving

306 cals	4.1g fiber
5.3g fat	0.1g salt
0.5g saturated fat	
53.2g sugar	**1.8g fat per 100g**

This recipe brings out the sweet, juicy flavor of a peach. I've left the skins on for fiber; if you want to remove them, make a small cut top and bottom and blanch in boiling water for 1 minute. Cool, then peel.

Serves 4

4 peaches, halved, pits removed
8 amaretti cookies
3 tablespoons dark brown sugar
2 tablespoons amaretto liqueur (optional)
1¼ cups (10 oz) fat-free Greek yogurt
2 tablespoons sifted confectioner's sugar
1 pint (8 oz) raspberries

Preheat the oven to 375°F.

Place the peaches cut-side up in a baking dish. Crumble the amaretti cookies in a bag with a rolling pin. You're not looking for a powder, just small chunks. Combine the cookies with the brown sugar, and liqueur if using.

Fill the peach cavities with the cookie mixture, place in the oven, and bake for 25 minutes, or until the peaches have softened and caramelized. Keep an eye out for burning. If so, reduce the oven temperature.

Meanwhile, place the yogurt in a bowl with the confectioner's sugar and raspberries, then whisk vigorously to break up the fruits, creating a pink, chunky sauce. Serve the cold raspberry sauce with the hot peaches.

Raspberry pancakes with blueberry sauce

Per serving
373 cals
4.8g fat
1.2g saturated fat
40.6g sugar

3.3g fiber
0.7g salt

1.7g fat per 100g

These pancakes are also great for lazy weekend breakfasts, but they make a delicious dessert and are especially loved by children.

Serves 6

1 large Granny Smith apple, peeled, quartered and cored, then roughly diced
3 tablespoons water
2 tablespoons lemon juice
4 tablespoons superfine sugar
1 free-range egg, separated
2 egg whites
2½ cups (20 oz) fat-free Greek yogurt
2¼ cups (9 oz) self-rising flour
1 pint (8 oz) raspberries, mashed with a fork
spray of vegetable oil

SAUCE:

1¼ cups (6 oz) blueberries, roughly chopped
4 tablespoons blackberry jam
1 tablespoon superfine sugar
1 tablespoon lime juice

Place the apple in a saucepan with the water, lemon juice, and half the sugar and cook over gentle heat until the apple breaks down to a purée, about 12–15 minutes. Allow to cool.

Beat the three egg whites to soft peaks, then add the remaining sugar and beat until the mixture is glossy and forms stiff peaks.

Beat together the egg yolk, apple purée, yogurt, flour, and crushed raspberries, then fold in one spoonful of beaten egg white to slacken the mixture before folding in the remaining egg whites.

Heat a large, nonstick frying pan and spray with oil. Drop tablespoons of raspberry batter onto the frying pan and cook for about 2 minutes until little bubbles appear on the surface. Flip over and cook for another minute. Keep warm in a cool oven. Cook until all the batter is used.

Meanwhile, make the sauce by placing all the ingredients in a saucepan and cooking for 3–4 minutes, stirring constantly. Serve it warm or hot, chunky or smooth. I like a chunky sauce, but feel free to blend it in a food processor.

Serve the pancakes with the blueberry sauce.

Tip

You can serve extra raspberries for a more substantial dessert.

Per serving (using 0% fat yogurt)

84 cals	2.8g fiber
0.2g fat	0g salt
0.1g saturated fat	
14.2g sugar	**0.1g fat per 100g**

Red fruits with Pedro Ximénez sherry

This is a fast, standby dessert that is really easy as long as you have the sherry. PX is a really chocolatey sherry, the flavor of which is unique; you'll have to search it out through the internet, or a good liquor store, but if you can't find it, a normal cream or sweet sherry will do, though it will be second best. On the health front, weight for weight, strawberries contain more vitamin C than citrus fruit.

Serves 4

1 pint (8 oz) strawberries, hulled and halved

1 pint (8 oz) raspberries

3 oz red currants, picked off the stalks (optional)

2 tablespoons Pedro Ximénez sherry

1 teaspoon chopped mint

2 teaspoons superfine sugar

4 tablespoons fat-free Greek yogurt

2 teaspoons lime juice

2 teaspoons honey

Combine the fruits with the sherry, mint, and sugar, and leave to macerate for 30 minutes.

Meanwhile, combine the yogurt with the lime juice and honey.

When ready to serve, divide the fruits between four glass bowls or tumblers, and top with a dollop of yogurt.

Tip

You could use low-fat crème fraîche instead of the yogurt, but note that this will increase the fat content quite considerably (above 3g per 100g), so save this one for a special treat.

Summer pudding

Per serving
220 cals 5.1g fiber
1.1g fat 0.5g salt
0.3g saturated fat
29.4g sugar **0.5g fat per 100g**

This delicious summer pudding is the perfect low-fat dessert.

Serves 8

4 pints (2 lb) raspberries
8 oz red currants, picked over
½ cup (2 oz) blackberries, picked over
scant ⅔ cup (4½ oz) superfine sugar
½ cup (4 fl oz) raspberry liqueur (such
    as crème de framboise), optional
10–12 slices of day-old whole grain
    bread, crusts removed
extra berries, to decorate

Sprinkle the fruit with the sugar and toss gently to combine. Cover and ideally leave to macerate for 2 hours.

Tip the fruit and resulting juices into a non-reactive saucepan with the liqueur and cook over medium heat for 3–4 minutes to release some more juices.

Meanwhile, line a 2-quart bowl with plastic wrap, then dip the bread into the fruit juices and lay on the plastic wrap, making sure that the slices of bread overlap slightly, and cover the sides and bottom of the bowl completely.

Using a slotted spoon, fill up the bread bowl with fruit. Pour over half the juices, then cover the fruit completely with more bread slices. Cover with plastic wrap, then top with a plate that fits inside the rim of the bowl. Place a heavy weight on top of the plate, and refrigerate overnight.

When you're ready to serve, turn the pudding over onto a shallow, but not flat, dish and remove the bowl and plastic wrap. Pour over the reserved juices, and serve with a few loose berries.

Saucy chocolate pudding

Per serving (based
on 8 servings)
273 cals 1g fiber
3.8g fat 0.4g salt
1.2g saturated fat
46.5g sugar **2.5g fat per 100g**

I used to eat a Betty Crocker version of this self-saucing pudding when I was a child and I found it fascinating that the sauce which started on the top ended up on the bottom...well, now I know.

Serves 6–8

4 tablespoons low-fat spread
½ cup (4 fl oz) skim milk
2 teaspoons coffee liqueur (optional)
¾ cup (6 oz) superfine sugar
1⅔ cups (5½ oz) self-rising flour
2 tablespoons unsweetened cocoa
    powder
¾ cup (6 oz) dark brown sugar
2 cups (17 fl oz) boiling water

Preheat the oven to 325°F. Lightly oil a baking dish that holds 1½ quarts and has sides approximately 1-inch deep.

Melt the spread in the milk over medium heat. Remove from the heat, then whisk in the liqueur, if using, the sugar, flour, and half the cocoa powder. Spoon the mixture into the baking dish.

Combine the sugar and remaining cocoa powder, sprinkle over the batter, then gently pour over the water Place in the oven, and bake for 50–60 minutes until firm. Remove from the oven and let it sit for 10 minutes before serving.

Apple and orange sponge pudding

Per serving

224 cals	3g fiber
2.7g fat	0.2g salt
0.7g saturated fat	
31.8g sugar	**1.3g fat per 100g**

Not steamed, but a similar effect, this pudding is low in fat so you can enjoy it without feeling guilty. Play around with the fruit content—so many combos work; apple and pear, apple and blackberry, apple and raspberry, mango and pineapple, and so on—the process remains the same.

Serves 6

2 medium Granny Smith apples, peeled, quartered and cored

2 McIntosh apples, peeled, quartered and cored

3 oranges, segmented, with juice squeezed from the membrane, keeping all the juice and the zest from 1 orange

3 tablespoons superfine sugar

¼ teaspoon ground cinnamon

2 tablespoons orange liqueur (optional)

2 free-range eggs

4 tablespoons superfine sugar

1 tablespoon cornstarch, sifted

1 tablespoon all-purrpose flour, sifted

3 tablespoons self-rising flour, sifted

Preheat the oven to 350°F.

Slice the apples and put in a saucepan with the juice from the oranges, 3 tablespoons sugar and ground cinnamon. Bring to a boil, cover with a lid, and cook for 12–15 minutes over medium heat. Stir in the orange liqueur, if using.

While the apples are cooking, make the sponge by beating the eggs and 4 tablespoons sugar together, ideally with an electric whisk for about 5 minutes, until pale and frothy. Fold in the sifted flours, and the orange zest.

Spoon the apple-orange mixture into a 1½ quart baking dish, then gently spread with the sponge. Bake in the oven for 30 minutes, or until the sponge is springy and golden. Serve with low-fat custard.

Per serving

340 cals	1.1g fiber
2.4g fat	0g salt
0.4g saturated fat	
81.4g sugar	**1.4g fat per 100g**

Toffee bananas

So simple, so popular, a crunchy toffee coating and a soft center—perfect with some low-fat fromage frais or ice cream.

Makes 12 sticks
Serves 4

3 ripe bananas, each peeled and cut into four on the diagonal

juice of 1 lemon

generous cup (9 oz) superfine sugar

½ cup (4 fl oz) water

1 tablespoon sesame seeds

Toss the bananas in the lemon juice to prevent discoloration and to add a little tartness. Place one banana piece on the end of a wooden skewer.

Place the sugar and water in a saucepan and warm over medium heat. Have a bowl of water with a pastry brush handy to brush the sides of the pan to prevent crystals forming. Cook until the caramel has reached a pale golden color, remove from the heat and swirl the pan gently.

Have another bowl of cold water on standby. Dip each banana into the caramel, hold for 30 seconds, then lift out, sprinkle with a few sesame seeds, and plunge for into the cold water to set the caramel.

Serve immediately.

Apple and blackberry brûlées

Per serving
249 cals   1.9g fiber
2.2g fat   0.3g salt
0.7g saturated fat
51.1g sugar   **0.7g fat per 100g**

We all need to spoil ourselves with a dessert from time to time, but low-fat versions of full-fat favorites can often be disappointing. This is based on a crème caramel recipe, but I've slashed the fat content by making a custard using skim milk and just one egg yolk with extra whites (which are fat-free).

Serves 4

6 tablespoons superfine sugar
   plus 1 tablespoon for glazing
2 tablespoons water
2 dessert apples, peeled, cored
   and diced
scant cup (4 oz) blackberries
1 whole egg
2 egg whites
2½ cups (20 fl oz) skim milk
grated nutmeg for dusting

Heat half the sugar and the 2 tablespoons of water in a saucepan until it starts to turn a golden caramel color, occasionally swirling the pan and brushing down the sides just above the sugar line with a wet brush.

Working quickly, (the sugar will turn from golden to bitter dark very quickly) add the apple and cook, stirring frequently, for 2 minutes. Fold in the blackberries, stirring to combine. Remove from the heat.

Meanwhile, whisk the egg with the egg whites until thoroughly combined.

Bring the milk to a boil, then whisk into the egg mix. Fold in the remaining sugar apart from the glazing sugar. Stir until the sugar has dissolved.

Preheat the oven to 325°F.

Spoon the apple mixture into the bottom of four ramekins, pour on the egg custard, and remove any bubbles from the surface with a teaspoon or paper towel. Then dust the surface with a little grated nutmeg.

Stand the ramekins in a deep roasting pan, and pour in enough hot water around them to come halfway up the sides.

Bake in the preheated oven for approximately 1 hour, or until set. Allow to cool, then refrigerate.

Sprinkle the tops with the superfine sugar for glazing, and use a blow-torch or hot broiler to caramelize the surface until golden with darker specks. **Do not refrigerate after glazing the surface.**

Tip

Try different fruits in the base; pear and walnut, raspberry and blueberry, pineapple and mango, or papaya and passion fruit.

A mid-morning snack

Per serving

208 cals   4.7g fiber

2.2g fat   0g salt

0.4g saturated fat

29.1g sugar   **2.9g fat per 100g**

We're all entitled to a snack, and yet so many are so high in fats, that often it's hard to find something suitable. I hope you'll enjoy this bar, but don't eat too many, as the dried fruits are high in sugar.

Makes 9

11 oz of your favorite dried fruits
   (I like dried apples, apricots, pears
   and blueberries)

7 oz nut-free muesli

½ teaspoon pumpkin pie spice

½ teaspoon ground cinnamon

¼ teaspoon Chinese five spice powder

⅔ cup (5 fl oz) hibiscus or
   pomegranate juice

2 tablespoons honey

⅔ cup (2 ½ oz) whole wheat flour

spray of oil

Pulse the dried fruit in a food processor until well chopped, but not puréed. Combine the fruit with the muesli and spices.

Meanwhile heat the juice and honey in a large saucepan, then stir in the flour, followed by the muesli mixture. Stir well to combine.

Preheat the oven to 400°F.

Line a 10-inch square or rectangular shallow baking dish with parchment paper and lightly spray with oil. Tip the mixture into the dish and smooth the top with a flat knife.

Bake in the oven for 25 minutes, checking from time to time to make sure it is not getting too brown; if it is, reduce the oven temperature to 350°F.

Allow to cool, turn out, then peel back the paper and cut into squares or rectangles, depending on the shape of your pan. Store in an airtight container for up to 1 week.

Tip

I'm going through a hibiscus drink phase, but feel free to use another juice such as apple.

Fruit bread biscotti

Per serving

22 cals	0.1g fiber
0g fat	0g salt
0g saturated fat	
3.4g sugar	**0.5g fat per 100g**

These brittle cookies are inspired by Italian biscotti, and are perfect served with a dessert, or even dipped in sweet wine.

Makes 50

3 egg whites
6 tablespoons (3 oz) superfine sugar
¼ teaspoon ground cinnamon
grated zest of 1 orange
1 cup (4 oz) all-purpose flour
¾ cup (4 oz) mixed dried fruit, chopped

Preheat the oven to 325°F.

Lightly oil the base and sides of a 10-inch rectangular shallow cake pan. Line with baking parchment paper, bringing the paper up and over the sides.

Using an electric whisk, beat the egg whites to soft peaks in a large bowl. With the whisk running, add the superfine sugar in a steady stream until the egg whites are glossy. With a spoon, fold in the remaining ingredients.

Spoon the mixture into the cake pan and smooth the top with a flat knife. Bake in the oven for 35 minutes until pale and golden. Allow to cool, then wrap in plastic wrap and leave overnight.

Preheat the oven to 275°F.

Turn the cookie out onto your worktop, and cut across the short side in very thin slices. Break the slices into different sized pieces and place on a wire rack. Return to the oven and bake for 15–20 minutes until crisp. Allow to cool, then store in an airtight container for up to one week.

Herby English scones

Per serving

118 cals	0.9g fiber
1.7g fat	0.9g salt
0.7g saturated fat	
1.6g sugar	**3g fat per 100g**

Makes 8

2 cups (8 oz) self-rising flour
1 teaspoon English mustard powder
½ teaspoon sweet paprika
½ teaspoon sea salt
1 hot red pepper, seeded and diced
2 teaspoons snipped chives
1 teaspoon finely chopped thyme
scant ½ cup (3½ oz) low-fat cream
    cheese
½ teaspoon finely chopped rosemary
2 teaspoons Worcestershire sauce
scant ½ cup (3½ oz) skim milk

Preheat the oven to 400°F.

Sift the flour, mustard, paprika, and salt into a bowl then add the pepper, chives, thyme, cream cheese, and rosemary, mixing well to combine.

Make a well in the center of the mixture, then add the Worcestershire sauce, and gradually add the milk, mixing until you have a soft dough. (You should have a little milk left over for brushing the scones before baking.)

Turn the dough out onto a floured surface, and gently knead to bring everything together. Roll out to about ¾-inch thickness, then stamp out your scones using a 2-inch plain cookie cutter. Collect up any dough trimmings, re-roll and stamp out a couple more.

Brush the scones with the saved milk, and place on a flat baking sheet. Place in the oven and bake for 15–18 minutes, or until risen and golden. Transfer to a wire rack to cool. Serve warm.

Tropical fruit cake

Per serving

237 cals   1.5g fiber

1.1g fat   0.5g salt

0.3g saturated fat

36.5g sugar   **1.2g fat per 100g**

Having two Aussie boys, I've grown used to their passion for carrot cake and banana cake. Now I've created one with lower fat and a lighter flavor which I hope they and you will enjoy. You can vary the dried fruits to suit your taste.

Serves 12

2⅔ cups (10¾ oz) all-purpose flour

½ teaspoon sea salt

2 teaspoons baking powder

¾ cup (6 oz) soft light brown sugar

½ teaspoon fresh grated ginger

1 free-range egg, beaten

pulp from 2 passion fruits

1 small ripe banana, mashed

⅔ cup (5 oz) low-fat fromage frais

3 oz dried mango, finely diced

3 oz dried pineapple, finely chopped

ICING:

1 cup (4 oz) confectioner's sugar, sifted

up to 2 teaspoons pineapple juice

Preheat the oven to 350°F.

Lightly oil a 7-inch round cake pan and line the bottom and sides with parchment paper.

Sift the flour, salt, and baking powder into a large bowl, then fold in the sugar, and stir well to combine. Make a large well in the center.

In a separate bowl, beat together the ginger, egg, passion fruit pulp, banana, and fromage frais, and pour into the well you've made in the flour. Using your hand, mix the wet and dry ingredients together, but without overworking it. Fold in the dried fruit.

Spoon the mixture into the cake pan and smooth the surface. Bake in the oven for about 50 minutes, or until a toothpick comes out clean. Allow to cool slightly, then turn out onto a wire rack.

Meanwhile, make the icing by mixing the confectioner's sugar with the pineapple juice, adding a little at a time to make a soft, but *not runny* icing. When the cake has cooled sufficiently, drizzle the icing over the cake in a random, streaky manner.

The cake will keep for four days if stored in an airtight container.

Baked apples with dried fruit

Per serving

246 cals	4.1g fiber
1g fat	0.1g salt
0g saturated fat	
55.7g sugar	**0.4g fat per 100g**

Granny Smiths are good cooking apples because they become really fluffy and souffléed when cooked. With the sugar, orange juice, and syrup, I have created a lovely toffee-ish sauce that will banish that yearning for cream or custard.

Serves 4

4 Granny Smith apples

2 tablespoons dried blueberries

2 tablespoons dried cherries

4 dried apricots

4 Medjool dates, pitted and chopped

⅓ cup rolled oats

½ teaspoon pumpkin pie spice

¼ teaspoon ground cinnamon

3 tablespoons dark brown sugar

⅓ cup (2½ fl oz) orange juice

1 tablespoon light corn syrup

Preheat the oven to 400°F.

Core the apples using an apple corer or melon baller; I find the latter works best as you want to get right inside the apple, and hollow out more of a cavity to accommodate more fruit. Then, using the tip of a sharp knife, score the skin centrally around the circumference of each apple to prevent them from bursting during baking.

Combine the fruits, oats, spices, and brown sugar in a bowl, then spoon into the cavity of the apples. If there is too much, just scatter into the baking pan.

Place the apples in the baking pan, then pour over the orange juice and corn syrup.

Bake for 45 minutes, basting every 10 minutes. Reduce the temperature to 350°F if the apples are browning too quickly.

Per serving

231 cals	3.4g fiber
0.3g fat	0g salt
0.1g saturated fat	
56.7g sugar	**0.2g fat per 100g**

Honey-broiled figs and friends

Figs are delicious, but misunderstood—they live with the legacy that they are good for constipation. Be that as it may, they are delicious in so many guises, both savory and sweet.

Serves 4

4 figs, halved through the stalk

1 mango, peeled, pitted and cut into several chunky slivers

2 sweet oranges, segmented (the juice from squeezing the membranes saved)

4 tablespoons superfine sugar

½ teaspoon ground cinnamon

6 tablespoons honey

1 tablespoon orange liqueur (optional)

2 oz pomegranate seeds

Arrange the figs, cut-side up, with the mango slivers and orange segments decoratively in a suitable baking dish. Combine the sugar and cinnamon and sprinkle over the fruit.

Place under the broiler and broil until the sugar is melted and bubbling, and the figs have browned.

Meanwhile, heat the saved orange juice and honey in a saucepan and bring to a boil. Reduce over medium heat until sticky, then fold in the orange liqueur, if using.

Serve the fruit piping hot, drizzled with the honey and orange liqueur, if using, and scattered with pomegranate seeds.

Dried fruit and ginger pudding

Per serving

341 cals   2.2g fiber

5.7g fat   0.8g salt

2.1g saturated fat

44.8g sugar   **2.6g fat per 100g**

Steamed puddings are such a treat—they cost very little to make, but they do require a little effort. The choice of fruits is very much down to you, the cook. Here I use dates, figs, and apple.

Serves 8

heaping ½ cup (3 oz) dried figs, finely chopped

¼ cup (1½ oz) dried apple, chopped

¼ cup (1½ oz) undyed candied cherries, chopped

¼ cup (1½ oz) stem ginger in syrup, chopped

4 tablespoons low-fat spread

½ cup (4 oz) dark brown sugar

4 tablespoons water

¾ cup (6 fl oz) skim milk

1 tablespoon malt vinegar

1½ teaspoons baking soda

1¾ cups (7 oz) all-purpose flour

½ teaspoon ground cinnamon

½ teaspoon ground ginger

1 teaspoon pumpkin pie spice

2 lb low-fat custard

Lightly oil a 2-quart pudding bowl and place a disc of baking parchment in the bottom.

Place the fruits and ginger in a saucepan with the low-fat spread, sugar, and water and heat until the fat has melted, then cool.

Place the milk in a saucepan, and bring to a boil. Add the vinegar and baking soda, and remove from the heat.

Sift the flour and spices into a bowl, mix to combine, then make a well in the center. Combine the milk with the dried fruit mixture and stir into the flour. Mix well, but don't overwork.

Pour the mixture into the pudding bowl, cover with a disc of baking parchment, then cover with oiled foil, and secure with string. Place the bowl in a saucepan and pour enough boiling water around the bowl to come three-quarters of the way up. Place a lid on the pan and boil for 1½–1¾ hours, or until firm. Top up the water level with boiling water as necessary.

Turn the pudding out onto a serving dish, and serve with low-fat custard.

Malted tea bread with blackberry and apple spread

Per serving
352 cals   6.9g fiber
2.9g fat   0.6g salt
0.1g saturated fat
48.2g sugar   **1.2g fat per 100g**

I love these sorts of loaves, which bring back childhood memories of tea with Gran. I mixed my dried fruits, but feel free to use the same quantities of whatever you have in your cupboard.

Serves 6–8

1⅓ cups (6 oz) rolled oats

½ cup (4 oz) dark brown sugar

½ teaspoon ground cinnamon

½ teaspoon pumpkin pie spice

½ cup (3 oz) dried blueberries

½ cup (3 oz) dried cherries

1¼ cups (5 oz) dried apricots, chopped

1¼ cups (10 fl oz) brewed and strained
   Earl Grey tea, cold

2 tablespoons malt extract

1½ cups (6 oz) self-rising whole
   wheat flour

½ teaspoon sea salt

1½ teaspoons baking powder

FRUIT SPREAD:

1½ cups (10 oz) blackberries

1 large Granny Smith apple, peeled,
   cored and chopped

1¼ cups (10 fl oz) unsweetened
   apple juice

Preheat the oven to 350°F and lightly oil and line a 9 x 5 x 3-inch loaf pan with parchment paper.

Place the rolled oats, sugar, cinnamon, pumpkin pie spice, and dried fruit in a bowl with the tea and malt extract. Soak for 1 hour, stirring from time to time.

Sift in the flour, salt, and baking powder, adding any bran that won't pass through the sieve. Bring the mixture together, but don't overwork.

Spoon into the lined pan, place in the oven and bake for 1½ hours, or until a toothpick comes out clean. Leave to cool for 15 minutes, then turn out onto a wire rack to cool completely.

Meanwhile, for the fruit spread, place all the ingredients in a saucepan and bring to a boil. Reduce the heat, and simmer until thick and very little liquid remains—you'll have to stir frequently. Push the fruit mixture through a sieve to remove the seeds, then allow to cool.

Serve slices of the bread with the spread.

Double rose and rosé gelatin with fresh raspberries

Per serving	
221 cals	1.4g fiber
0.2g fat	0g salt
0.1g saturated fat	
33.5g sugar	**0.1g fat per 100g**

Pink is very much the color of summer, so this refreshing dessert is perfect for outdoor dining, plus jelly is the ultimate fat-free dessert! As the raspberries are not set into the gelatin, you may prefer to substitute strawberries or blueberries. For those not on a low-fat diet you may like to offer some heavy cream...Oh dear, I'm such a tease!!

Serves 6

25 fl oz bottle of your favorite
   rosé wine
²⁄₃ cup (5 oz) superfine sugar
1 cup (8 fl oz) water
1 tablespoon rosewater
2 tablespoons raspberry liqueur
   (optional)
8 unflavored gelatin sheets
1½ pints (12 oz) fresh raspberries
a handful of unsprayed rose petals
   (optional)

Put the rosé wine, superfine sugar, and water into a saucepan, bring to a boil, reduce the heat and simmer for 5 minutes. (The sugar will dissolve before boiling, but to get a really sparkling gelatin, follow my instructions.) Remove from the heat and fold in the rosewater and liqueur if using.

Meanwhile, soften the gelatin sheets in plenty of cold water until the sheets swell (bloom), then drain, and squeeze out as much excess liquid as you can. Stir the gelatin into the hot rosé liquid, cover and place in the refrigerator to set.

Once the jelly has set completely, using a knife, chop the gelatin in the bowl until you have a shimmering pile of gelatin.

Alternatively, spoon the loose gelatin and the raspberries into glasses and garnish with unsprayed rose petals.

Passion fruit and mango soufflés

Per serving	
196 cals	1.4g fiber
3.5g fat	0.2g salt
1g saturated fat	
32.7g sugar	**2.7g fat per 100g**

Everyone is scared of a soufflé, but it's truly just a case of following the basics. This soufflé is a very light offering, without a roux base, so eat it as soon as it comes out of the oven. It would go nicely with a dollop of passion fruit sorbet.

Serves 4

1 tablespoon superfine sugar, plus
   extra for dusting
½ mango, peeled, cored and
   finely chopped
2 egg yolks
7 passion fruit, sieved to remove seeds
2 tablespoons vodka (optional)
¾ cup (3 oz) confectioner's sugar
4 egg whites, room temperature

Preheat the oven to 400°F. Lightly grease four soufflé ramekins, then dust with superfine sugar, and divide the mango between the dishes.

Whisk the egg yolks with the passion fruit purée, vodka (if using) and a third of the confectioner's sugar until frothy and well-combined.

Beat the egg whites at room temperature in a very clean bowl. When soft peaks are reached, gradually beat in the remaining sugar until the egg whites are glossy and stiff. Fold one spoonful of the egg white into the passion fruit to slacken the mixture, then carefully fold in the remainder.

Spoon the mixture into the soufflé dishes, then run your thumb around the rim to help an even rise. Bake in the oven for 12–14 minutes until golden and risen. Remove from the oven, dust with confectioner's sugar and serve.

Baked summer fruit bundles

Per serving	
179 cals	3.2g fiber
0.2g fat	0.1g salt
0g saturated fat	
27.2g sugar	**0.1g fat per 100g**

I love warm fruit, even in the height of summer. Heating fruit brings out its natural aromas and sweetness. Too often, many of our store-bought fruits are picked underripe, and are pretty tasteless; this recipe addresses that problem, and makes for a delicious dessert.

Serves 4

12½ fl oz orange Muscat dessert wine

2 tablespoons honey

1 bay leaf

grated zest and juice of 1 orange

1 vanilla bean, split and scraped to remove seeds (don't discard!)

4 thick slices of orange, seeds, rind, and pith removed

½ pint (4 oz) raspberries

⅓ cup (2 oz) blueberries

1 peach, pitted, and cut into 4 wedges

1 nectarine, pitted and cut into 4 wedges

⅓ cup blackberries, stems removed

4 dried apricots, diced

Preheat the oven to 350°F.

Put the wine, honey, bay leaf, orange zest and juice, and vanilla bean and seeds in a saucepan and heat until simmering, then turn off the heat and allow to infuse for 15 minutes.

Combine all the fruits in a bowl. Cut out four pieces of parchment paper, roughly 12 inches square. Wet one of the pieces and place in a small bowl, leaving enough overlapping to create a bundle.

Spoon a quarter of the fruit mixture into the parchment paper, making sure that some of each fruit is included. Cut the vanilla bean into four and place one piece in the bundle with the fruit. Pour in a quarter of the infused liquid. Gather up the overhanging parchment paper, creating a money purse, and tie tightly with string. Set aside and repeat with the other three bundles.

Arrange the bundles on a baking sheet and bake for 15 minutes.

Serve the bundles hot so that your fellow diners can unwrap their own, releasing a beautiful aroma.

Tip

You can play around with the fruit. In autumn, orchard fruits would work well, but allow a slightly longer cooking time in order to soften the apples and pears. If serving this dessert to children, replace the wine with orange or apple juice.

Apricot meringue fool

Per serving

273 cals   4.8g fiber

0.6g fat   0.2g salt

0g saturated fat

63.9g sugar   **0.5g fat per 100g**

A classic British dessert, which is based on Eton Mess, but without the whipped cream. Stem ginger adds a little unusual interest, and the wheat germ adds some extra fiber.

Serves 4

2 balls (1 oz) stem ginger in syrup, drained and finely chopped

8 oz dried apricots, finely diced

2 tablespoons wheat germ

3 fl oz water

2 egg whites, ideally pasteurized

3 tablespoons superfine sugar

3 store-bought or homemade meringue nests, crumbled

2 tablespoons loose-set apricot jam

Put the ginger, apricots, and wheat germ with the water in a small saucepan. Cook, covered, over low heat for 5 minutes, stirring from time to time to make sure that nothing is sticking, and the water hasn't evaporated. Remove from the heat, and allow to cool completely.

Place the egg whites in a very clean bowl and beat to soft peaks using an electric whisk, or a balloon whisk plus plenty of elbow grease. Add the sugar, and continue to beat for about 2–3 minutes, until stiff and glossy.

Carefully fold the apricot mixture into the glossy egg whites, then fold in the broken meringues. Spoon into four chilled glasses, then drizzle with a little apricot jam. Serve immediately.

Tip

If you haven't got loose-set apricot jam, you can simply heat set jam to loosen it, or alternatively, use a drizzle of honey.

Orange and lemon Eton mess

Per serving

180 cals   1.1g fiber

0.6g fat   0.1g salt

0.2g saturated fat

27.4g sugar   **0.3g fat per 100g**

Eton mess is one of the best-selling desserts in our restaurants, and in this low-fat version, I'm using fat-free yogurt.

Serves 4

3 store-bought or homemade meringue nests

2 tablespoons low-fat lemon curd

2 oranges, zest grated, then segmented

2 cups (1 lb) fat-free Greek yogurt

2 tablespoons Limoncello (lemon liqueur)

TO SERVE:

grated zest of 1 orange

sprig of mint

Crumble half the meringue nests into four glasses, and drizzle with half the lemon curd, then add half the orange segments.

Combine the orange zest with the yogurt and lemon liqueur, then spoon half into the glasses. Repeat the layers, finishing with the yogurt.

Garnish with more grated orange zest and a mint sprig.

Index

Acknowledgments

I'd like to mention a few people who have helped me create this book:

To my wonderful wife, Jacinta and our two children, Toby and Billie, who continue to give me support and encouragement and without whom, life would be very different.

To Louise Townsend, my energetic and ultra-efficient PA who enthusiastically plowed her way through my handwritten recipes.

To Fiona Lindsay, Mary, Alison and Mac at Limelight Management who keep me busy.

To my team at my pub The Greyhound in Oxfordshire who were on hand to stand in when deadlines loomed nearer, and I had to depart from my usual place in the kitchens.

And to Judith Hannam, my excellent editor and her great team, including: designer Jacqui Caulton and home economist Aya Nishimura. Georgia Glynn Smith, the photographer of this book, also deserves a mention; a great creative talent who has a real eye for bringing food to life on the pages of this book. And not forgetting the significant contribution of nutritionist, Juliette Kellow, who analyzed all my recipes and made suggestions where needed.

And finally to all of those out there who have been asking for this book—here it is! Whether your reason to pick up this book is for weight loss, or specific advice from a health professional to eat less fat in your diet, I hope I've given you inspiration that all is not lost, apart from the fat . . .